Haunted Austin, Texas

Haunted Austin, Texas
-Cold Spots-

Scott A. Johnson

Schiffer Publishing Ltd®

4880 Lower Valley Road, Atglen, Pennsylvania 19310

Schiffer Books are available at special discounts for bulk purchases for sales promotions or premiums. Special editions, including personalized covers, corporate imprints, and excerpts can be created in large quantities for special needs. For more information contact the publisher:

Published by Schiffer Publishing Ltd.
4880 Lower Valley Road
Atglen, PA 19310
Phone: (610) 593-1777;
Fax: (610) 593-2002
E-mail: Info@schifferbooks.com

For the largest selection of fine reference books on this and related subjects, please visit our web site at:
www.schifferbooks.com
We are always looking for people to write books on new and related subjects. If you have an idea for a book please contact us at the above address.

This book may be purchased from the publisher.
Include $5.00 for shipping.
Please try your bookstore first.
You may write for a free catalog.

In Europe, Schiffer books are distributed by
Bushwood Books
6 Marksbury Ave.
Kew Gardens
Surrey TW9 4JF England
Phone: 44 (0) 20 8392 8585; Fax: 44 (0)
20 8392 9876
E-mail: info@bushwoodbooks.co.uk
Website: **www.bushwoodbooks.co.uk**

Acknowledgments

So many people were instrumental in making this book a reality, and thanks must be given where it is due. First, to my wife and children, for indulging me in this strange and macabre fascination; to Steve Barton, Debbi Moore, Johnny Butane, Buz, Morgan, Nomad, and the other Dread Central guys for giving me my first outlet for real ghost stories; to Clint, Heather, Matt, Hoshi, Tiff, and Marchelle, my fellow members of Cold Spots Paranormal Research; and to the rest of my family, who's strange and wonderful history gave me the background to appreciate these stories.

However, in researching stories such as these, there is only so much a person can find. There are stories in every city about things being haunted that are unsubstantiated, and often these places turn out to be victims of rumor or urban legend. It is for this reason that researchers seek out people who've experienced the hauntings, historians, and others who are just plain helpful. To that end, the author would like to thank:

Abby, from David Grimes Photography Studio,
and David Grimes, for his willingness to share
his stories;
Lesha Gonzolez, of the Old Spaghetti Ware-
house;
Phoebe Williams, of Carrington's Bluff;
Ryan Fulmer, of the Bitter End Bar and
Brewery;
Barbara Allen, of University of Texas, Austin;
Cecille Marcato, of the Neill-Cochran House
Museum;
Lillian Beckwidth, of the Austin Club;
Janine Plummer, of Austin Ghost Tours;
Donna Hays, of the Austin Women's Club;
Tony Johnson, of the Paramount Theater;
Kevin Legrow, of Speakeasy's;
Saundra Turner, of the Austin Convention &
Visitors Bureau;
Ed VanDeVort, Local Historian;
Mischell Amadore and Dianne Brownlee, of
St. Edwards University;
Clayton Stapleton, of What Was Then;
The Austin American Statesman
The Atchison Globe, November 19, 1888

Also, many thanks must go to the folks at St. Edward's University for
allowing me access to their university archives for fact-checking.

Contents

Foreword

What makes a place haunted? No matter where I go or what age group I'm speaking to, the question comes up again and again. Most of the time, I try my best to answer the question, but there are just too many "causes" for me to try to pinpoint a single action that defines why one house is haunted and another isn't. A horrifically violent death may be the cause of one, but other places with a similar history may not be haunted. Spirits, according to some cultures and faiths, are around us all the time, so what is it that earns a house or building the distinction of being haunted? Wherever emotions run high...wherever there is unrest due to unsolved issues, the grounds are fertile for a haunting. It isn't just pain that causes them, but in many cases love, joy, or even sorrow can leave an imprint—a lasting mark on the brick and mortar, even in the soil itself. While every place has a history, they all don't have one so wild and wooly as Texas.

There is something about the Texas Hill Country that speaks to visitors. Whether in or outside city limits, one cannot help but be taken in by the beauty and history of the landscape. There is, for lack of a better word, a type of magic that steals the breath away, and which exists in no other state of the union. Nowhere is the bewitching power of Texas more apparent than its capital, Austin. From the impressive architecture of the inner city to the lush greenery of the parks and outlying areas, the appeal of the city is undeniable.

In addition to being the Texas state capital, Austin is often referred to as the "live music capital of the world," and is considered the proving ground for up-and-coming musicians of all genres. It holds several museums, beautiful lakes, parks, theaters, comedy troops, golf courses, and hundreds of other points of fascinating interest, providing tourists with endless diversions on any day of the week. For the more academically minded, there seems to be a college around nearly every corner. And proudly displayed across countless car bumpers and t-shirts is a motto by which many Austinites live: "Keep Austin Weird." It is, however, best known for its nightlife, in which music scorches the air while patrons dance to varying rhythms along 6th Street.

There is, however, another side of Austin that many don't see. As the sun sinks below the horizon, nature buffs set up cameras and binoculars on the banks of Town Lake in hopes of catching the mass exodus of bats that pour from under the Town Lake Bridge, the largest such urban population in America. And while the bats take wing into the night sky, there are places where voices are heard from empty rooms, where screams echo in the night, and where the dead simply refuse to stay buried. Every night that passes gives chilling insight to the history of this historic city, and proves that the land, no matter how modern, doesn't forget.

The purpose of this book is to serve as an odd sort of "guide book" for those who seek out places where the shadows run colder and where the darkness is thick as tar. While it might surprise some, others will realize that not every place that looks haunted is haunted, and many places that seem benign have their share of permanent residents. Some aficionados will note that the places marked herein are not quite a complete list, missing a home here, and a building there. The reasons behind the purposeful omissions are varied, but simple. In some cases, the haunted site simply doesn't exist anymore, a victim of a developer's wrecking ball. In other cases, activity seems to have ceased. As this book's purpose is to guide people to active spots, their inclusion seemed unnecessary. Most omissions, however, were made for the simple reason that the current owners of the property asked that their site not be included. Whether because the activity has ceased or because they simply don't want the kind of attention that owning a haunted building can garner, their wishes must be respected.

It should also be noted that, while the author has made every effort to document the best times to *perhaps* catch a glimpse of something strange in each location, ghosts are not paid performers, trained monkeys, or even particularly adherent to time-tables. Put simply, a person could visit every site in this book at the times mentioned, and never see a thing. For some, however, a chance encounter might garner the most hair-raising experience of their lives.

Walking down the streets of Austin, look around, take in the sights, breathe in the aromas. See the buildings as what they were in times gone by, and remember those who came before. It is for this reason, above all others, that this book was written.

1

The Haunted Halls of Government

A nation, no matter how great, is made by its people. From the first explorers to the most modern citizens, nations are made off the sweat of the brows of its people and by the strength of their backs. Nowhere is this truer than in Texas, whose landscape is unique in that it holds every climate, every terrain, and some of the deadliest creatures known to mankind. From the beginning, people chose their leaders and exalted them, building monuments to some of the greatest explorers and bravest men of their time. Those who shone brighter, whose visionary leadership helped to forge the republic and the state, became more than just individuals—they came to *represent* the people. Though not always perfect, Texans have always been proud of their senators and congressmen, a fact made evident by the elaborate structures made to house them.

Still, in every government, there are secrets. Within the hallowed halls, success was tempered by tragedy and greatness by loss. Some would say it was a futile attempt by fate to keep those proud Texans humble. Those past worries and pains still live on today, hidden away in shadows, existing only as whispers and a cool breeze that comes from seemingly nowhere. Those shades exist as reminders of the past and to ensure a brighter future. When the dead speak, many listen. Even in the highest office in the state, the past is never truly at rest.

The State Capitol Building

11th Street and Congress Avenue

D riving up Congress Avenue in downtown Austin can be a strange experience. On both sides of the street, there are signs of the modern times, brightly lit with neon, but ahead something seems wonderfully out of place. It's as if a palace rises up from the urban city streets, imposing in both size and structure. Ornately carved of red granite, its domed roof reaches high into the sky, topped with a statue of a woman who has reached for over a hundred years to place the star she holds into the heavens. Inside, the building is no less impressive, elegantly decorated with all the regality that befits the Capital's station. Taken in by a piece of artwork or furniture, a visitor asks a strangely dressed gentleman its origin...only to watch, stunned, as the man smiles, tips his hat, and walks *through* a neighboring wall.

Though Austin is a city proud of its accomplishments and residents, there are dark parts of its history that have left marks. Lest anyone forget, Austin was, at one time, a wild city, full of rowdy types and those to whom the law mattered little. As there are today, there were disagreements between gentlemen, but today, such arguments are seldom settled with a gun.

The Texas State Capitol Building

Its History

The massive structure was begun in 1885, a tremendous undertaking that employed hundreds of people for its construction alone. The builder, proud to be a citizen of the state, used nothing but materials widely available in Texas. His first choice for the walls was limestone, as such rocks can be found anywhere in the Texas hill country. However, after it was pointed out that two limestone structures had burned down in other parts of the state, the builder went to his alternative plan: red granite, all mined from Texas quarries, was chosen instead, adding a distinctive look and a certain desirable resistance to flames.

Even before construction began, rumors about the land on which the new capitol would stand were prevalent. People whispered about sightings of a young scout, one of the first to explore the Texas hill country, wandering the grounds aimlessly with his Indian maiden lover in tow. The scout, according to legend, died for his affair with the Indian girl at the hands of the Comanche chief and the maiden took her own life with a knife. Whether true or not, this Wild West love story persisted, leading many to believe the land—and therefore the capitol—was cursed from the beginning.

Construction on the palatial building lasted three years, opening in 1888. Though there are no confirmed reports of any tragic deaths occurring during construction, there are a few stories that tell about workers who gave their lives in the building of the most impressive structure in the city. According to some unconfirmed stories, men were crushed by falling stones and left where they died, with walls being built right on top of their still-warm corpses. When complete, the high dome and wide hallways confirmed the old adage—that things really are bigger in Texas.

The Capitol Building has, over the years, witnessed many strange and historic events that shaped the state and, in turn, the nation. However, it was in 1903, five years after its doors first opened, that the building had its first confirmed death.

On the morning of June 30, a former employee of the state comptroller's department, W. G. Hill, arrived at his former place of business with a gun in his hand. He walked up to the desk of Robert Marshall Love and shot him. His motives for the murder were never made clear, as even Love was quoted as saying, "I have no idea why he shot me." He died hours later of his wound, forgiving his assassin with his dying breath.

In the 1980s, death again visited the State Capitol, this time in the form of a suicide. While the name of the victim is unknown, there seems to be a general consensus that the event did, in fact, take place, and is not just a fanciful urban legend.

The Ghosts

Ghost stories in the halls of government are nothing new, as every state capital and building in Washington D.C. seems to have at least a few stories. Many can be chalked up to overactive imaginations or light-hearted rumors. Some, however, defy rational explanation, resisting the bonds of logic. While many stories ring more of poetic minds than hard evidence, there are others that simply won't be denied.

Though there are romantic stories involving former state officials, explorers, and entire ghost congregations in the hallowed halls, there are only four that appear with any regularity—and the number of people who have seen them numbers in the hundreds. They range from tourists and employees to believers and skeptics. Every background and educational level is represented in the reporting body, showing that the dead have no preference to whom they show themselves... only that they're looking for a listening ear.

Security guards are often asked about the kindly gentleman whose clothes are out of place. He rarely, if ever speaks, but he will doff his hat and smile broadly. When asked a question, or when approached by security guards, the man always has the same reaction. He simply turns and walks through a nearby wall. He has been identified as

Robert Love, the unfortunate man who was murdered for no apparent reason. He has been seen watching people from the second floor, and has also been caught on video surveillance cameras.

Another interesting sighting occurs in the rotunda. Visitors and employees alike have reported seeing a man wandering aimlessly about...*until he vanishes before their eyes*. According to those who have worked there for more than twenty years, the man committed suicide in the building in the 1980s. Though his name seems to have been lost to time, his soul has not been at rest since.

Perhaps the oldest and most enduring sighting, recorded since *before* the building stood, is that of the young scout and his Indian bride. Even today, the ill-fated lovers roam the grounds, occasionally startling employees, security guards, and visitors alike. Far from being frightened, many who see them find their story to be both romantic and tragically beautiful.

In addition to the sightings, paranormal investigators have recorded a number of *Electronic Voice Phenomena*, voices of those long since dead captured on tape recorder but usually not heard at the time it was being said. Recordings of voices that say, "Senator...let's run him!" and "Thank you, Frank" are among the most clear, but not every spirit inside the Capitol is benign. At least one voice recorded referred to a half-Native American investigator as a "half breed."

Present Day

The State Capitol building still stands—the largest of its kind in the United States—and is still a very busy place. Lawmakers and lobbyists roam the halls at any given time, as do tour groups of out-of-state visitors and students. And still, despite the updated wiring and the trappings of modern technology within the old walls, the hauntings continue. It seems every week there are reports of some curious thing happening that defies logic. The guards dutifully report each incident, all the while knowing full well just who and what roams the halls of the State Capitol. The restless souls are so widely known that walking ghost tours of the downtown area feature the State Capitol.

During regular hours, and often into the night, the State Capitol bustles with the everyday business of running a state. Daily tours are available. The yard is particularly beautiful during the spring months, when the flowers are in bloom.

The Texas State Capitol, while imposing and grand during the daylight hours, is breathtaking at night. Against the Austin skyline, the dome is lit from all around, giving it a glow that shouts of Texas pride.

Three of the four ghosts that haunt the building have no regular schedule that they adhere to, but rather are prone to popping up at unexpected times throughout the year. However, Robert Love seems to revisit his workplace more during the month of June, around the anniversary of his death, than any other.

††††††

For more information, call the Visitor's Center at 512-305-8400. To arrange a tour, call 512-463-0063. For information about the inner workings of the building, visit the web site, http://www.texasonline.com.

The Governor's Mansion

Corner of 11th Street and Colorado Avenue

Within sight of the State Capitol building, school children in their uniformed white shirts and blue slacks stand in line around a stately mansion. Some fidget in line while others listen attentively to what their teacher or guide is saying. Seen from outside the gates, the Governor's Mansion is a beautiful design; Greek Revival with high pillars and a sleeping porch, low hanging shade trees, and regal steps that perfectly fit the station of the man who lives within. Inside the gates, however, the air is hushed. The quiet is only partially out of respect for the office and out of reverence for this living piece of history. The other part, however, may be due to a cold chill that may occasionally whip through the air, even in the midst of summer, and some swear they are being watched.

There are many types of hauntings, each with its own cause and manifestations. In some cases, a haunting can be caused by a personality so big it leaves an imprint on the brick and mortar...an echo that remains until the walls are gone and sometimes beyond. For others, it is tragedy; a life cut short, or even heartbreak. The Governor's Mansion is a rarity in the world of the supernatural, for while both types of hauntings are common, they are rarely found together.

The Governor's Mansion

Its History

For nine years, Texas Governors lived in standard housing along with the citizens of the city. However, those in power felt that the man who held the state's highest title should have a suitable residence, one with regality, to fit his station. So, in 1854, master builder Abner Hugh Cook drew up plans for a home fit for a king. The walls were to be made from bricks from a clay pit on the Colorado River. Timbers were to be cut by the sawmill in nearby Bastrop. The fact that Cook owned both his suppliers was not lost on anyone. After two years, the building was completed.

The mansion proved to be all Cook had designed it to be, providing luxurious living accommodations for several that held the office.

Three years after its completion, Texas legend Sam Houston assumed the office of Governor and took up residence in the mansion. The former Republic of Texas President and hero held the office for only two years.

Several years later, Pendleton Murrah was elected Governor. He was only in office for a year before tragedy struck in the form of a suicide within his home. In 1864, it was common for relatives to stay with their more affluent family members. Staying in the mansion at the time were at least two relatives, a niece and nephew from different sides of the family. The boy, nineteen years old and impetuous, soon became smitten with his cousin's beauty. He proposed marriage to her, only to have the girl reject his advances. Grief stricken and broken hearted, the young boy retired to his upstairs bedroom, where he shot himself.

Since those early days, many have assumed the title of Governor of Texas. Those that lived within the mansion's walls claim that, while the home befits the station and is all a person could ask for, all is not right...as the dead tend to roam the halls and peek from behind doors when all is quiet in the stillness of the night.

The Ghosts

Over the years, there have been a great many reports of strange happenings and phenomena in the house from both residents and tourists. The causes of the hauntings are well known—as are the identities of the restless spirits.

The first ghost is thought to be an echo of a powerful personality that governed the land, Texas legend Sam Houston. Seen most often in his old bedroom, he has startled many over the years. Even as late as the 1980s, his presence was marked in his old home. The wife and daughter of 1980s Texas Governor Mark White claimed to have had many encounters with the giant Texan. In fact, they had so many run-ins with the apparition that they eventually began referring to him simply as "old Sam."

Tragedy and high emotions are believed to be at the cause of the second haunting, as the halls are still walked by the impetuous nephew of Governor Murrah. Even in modern times, with the house awash with a constant river of tourists, reports come in of strange activity concerning the boy's spirit. Footsteps are heard in his former bedroom, along with the sound of lovelorn cries. Many have visited the room only to step into a cold spot that chills them to the bone and fills them with a feeling of sadness. Perhaps the most eerie occurrence is that the doorknobs in the mansion turn when there is no one on the other side of the door. Occasionally, doors intentionally left open will slam shut as if thrown by some unseen hand.

Present Day

Even now, more than a century after the mansion's construction, reports come in about residents who never left. Its great white pillars still have the ability to steal the breath away in awe and the lawn is meticulously kept. Still, there are times when the windows are not empty...when a giant of a Texas legend stares out at the strangers in his yard.

†††††

The mansion is open to visitors Monday through Thursday every week from 10 a.m. to noon, with tours scheduled every twenty minutes. It is a popular attraction for both historians and students alike. However, the spirits of the dead are most often seen when it is quiet—*after* the last tour has finished. To find the most definitive information, one needs only to visit the Friends of the Governor's Mansion online at http://www.txfgm.org, or by calling 512-474-9960.

2

Haunted Hotels

Sightseers in Austin have a rich palate from which to sample. Around every corner, there appears to be something new; some sight or sound or taste or smell that leaves visitors breathless and wishing they could never leave. Trying to take it all in, whether in a few days or weeks, is an exhausting, Herculean task. No matter how much good food a person loves or how well the bands play, the human body can only take so much until it needs to recharge. For some, any bed will do, so long as the sheets are clean and the hotel serves a continental breakfast. For others, though, their choice of lodging is as much a part of the experience as any club on 6th Street.

Horror scribe Stephen King once posed the question of hotel rooms: Do people think about what happened in that room before they stayed there? In certain places in Austin, one needn't wonder. The echoes of the past replay themselves time and time again, telling their stories of tragedy and pride for any lucky enough to see them. While none of the restless souls are harmful, they do add another level of adventure for guests of the city—and provide a glimpse into what came before.

The Driskill Hotel

604 Brazos Street

Towering over the city street, among the glass and neon that marks the modern world, stands a gothic masterpiece. With its regal air, broad verandas, marble floors, and beautiful chandeliers, one might assume the building to be a Texas castle, built by royalty of the Texas hill country. While the notion does fit, and the builder was considered southern royalty, it is in fact the grandest of the old hotels in Austin. And, as one could expect from such a lavish palace, some guests just don't seem to want to leave.

The Driskill has long been referred to as the most haunted hotel in the state, with decisions split between it and San Antonio's Menger Hotel in a friendly rivalry. Its history is so entwined with the city's that it seems that as the city became a reality so did it. As with any structure of its age, the walls and hallways of the Driskill have seen their share of tragedy—and the echoes of those events still resonate, startling guests and employees alike.

Its History

When cattle baron Jesse Lincoln Driskill bought an entire city block for $7,500, many thought him mad. His idea to build the grandest hostelry seemed to fit with the city plan, but even so, it was a large parcel of land and a great deal of money. However, when the structure opened to the public December 20, 1886, none could deny his vision. Though the structure's price came in at a whopping $400,000, it was

The Driskill Hotel

evident the money was well spent. Designed by Austin's own Jasper N. Preston and Sons, the hotel became the centerpiece to the streets on which it stood, inspiring awe in any who saw it. Driskill was so proud of his "frontier queen" that he had busts of himself and his two sons, Tobe and Bud, installed around the top of every entrance, making certain that anyone who crossed the threshold knew whose hotel it was.

Over the years, the old building has borne witness to many historical events and played host to some of the most important figures in Texas and American history. U.S. senators, presidents, and captains of industry have stayed in its lavish suites. The year 1898 saw the first long-distance telephone call in Austin placed from the Driskill's lobby, and years later, President Lyndon Banes Johnson watched election returns while relaxing in comfort.

When Driskill died, he left behind a remarkable landmark and a legacy of extravagance that continues to this day. While it catered to the upper crust, and life within its walls seemed almost like a fairytale, the hotel was unable to avoid tragedy for long.

Several deaths have occurred at the Driskill over the years. The first was the tragic demise of the four-year-old daughter of a U.S. Senator. The little girl was bright and bubbly, reportedly a delight to any who met her. On one particular afternoon, however, the child slipped while playing with a ball at the top of the grand staircase. She fell to the marble floor where she died.

The Driskill has also played host to functions of celebration, both public and private, in its extravagant ballrooms. It was during one such celebration that tragedy once again visited the hotel. A wedding that was to take place in the hotel was canceled the night before by the groom. Heartbroken, the young bride fled to her room...where she took her own life by hanging.

As the years went by, the Driskill, mirroring the state of the city around it, fell into disrepair. However, in the early 1990s, renovations began to restore it to its former glory. It was during this time that a woman from Houston checked into room 29 with a hauntingly familiar story. She'd come to Austin to rest her nerves after her fiancé cancelled their marriage at the last minute, and spent all of her first day in town on an extravagant shopping spree, using her fiancé's credit cards. She was last seen coming out of the elevator, headed to room 29, her arms overflowing with packages. When she did not reappear after three days, worry set in. The housekeepers opened the room and discovered her lifeless body, the victim of a self-inflicted gunshot wound to the stomach. According to police reports, the woman muffled the sound of the pistol with one of the hotel pillows. As such a wound rarely yields a fast death, it seemed she slowly suffered and bled to death over the course of the three days.

Its Ghosts

There are far too many restless souls inside the Driskill Hotel to identify. Some estimations place the number at just under a dozen while others soar into the twenties or even thirties. Even though the apparitions are as varied and diverse as the people who lodge there, there are at least six permanent guests that are reported with alarming frequency.

† Perhaps the most innocuous spirit is the one that most people only see at a glance. Believed to be Peter J. Lawless, he follows the same pattern day after day. Lawless actually lived in the hotel for thirty years, from 1886 to 1916—even when the hotel was closed to guests. Today, guests report seeing a man in old fashioned clothing standing outside the elevator, checking his watch. When they look back, the man is no longer there. Why he haunts the Driskill is a mystery.

† One spirit whose identity is of no doubt to anyone is that of Colonel Driskill himself. Most often, it's the heavy scent of cigar smoke that betrays his presence as he continues to inspect the building that bears his name. He has been reported on every floor,

but seldom interacts with guests or employees. On the top floor, however, the Colonel is most often blamed for bathroom lights in guests' rooms flipping on and off unaided.

† Walking down the grand staircase, one feels a chill as the third restless soul makes her presence known. Many have heard the plucky four-year-old bouncing her ball and giggling...only to turn and find the staircase empty. It's believed that she still plays on the stairs that claimed her life—and will occasionally tease guests with touches that are followed by her muffled giggles.

† The first bride to take her own life in the hotel, it seems, never left, and is one of the more active souls. She is most commonly seen on the fourth floor, still wearing her wedding gown. Though she's been seen occasionally by tourists, she also appears to guests who are at the hotel attending a wedding themselves, and has made her presence known at many a bachelorette party. Though her presence is steeped in tragedy, it is supposed to be good luck for the bride-to-be to see her.

† Not every spirit that haunts the hotel came from an untimely demise. One apparition, referred to as Mrs. Bridges, worked the front desk at the Driskill for many years. After her death, many reported that she still fussed over flower arrangements that were no longer there...and waited patiently behind the desk until someone came to relieve her from duty.

† Perhaps the most famous apparition is that of the so-called "Houston Bride." Most often spotted on the elevator, the lovely young woman is still seen carrying her parcels to room 29 before retiring for eternity. Many who see her are often unaware that the person they've just been talking to is not, in fact, flesh and bone. One pair of witnesses saw her while the building was being renovated—they watched as she stepped off on the fourth floor, which was draped in plastic, produced a key, and entered her room. Curious, the two went up to the room the next day and found that it was still in a state of renovation. The furniture had not even been placed in the room yet.

Present Day

The Driskill Hotel has become a haven for luxury travelers. The hotel itself instills a sense of grandeur to any who pass though its doors and awe to those who see it from the street. Apparitions are still seen, and quite frequently; though many of the hotel staff refuse to speak of their spectral guests.

No matter the time of year, the Driskill Hotel treats its guests to a luxurious stay. Reports of sightings occur year-round, with curious events occurring on nearly every level of the mammoth structure. Springtime, however, may just be the best time to stay, as the annual South-by-Southwest music festival happens all along 6th Street, and is within easy walking distance of the hotel.

†††††

To make reservations, guests can call toll-free at 800-252-9367, or visit the Driskill online at www.driskillhotel.com.

Carrington's Bluff

1900 David Street

Not every haunting is steeped in tragedy, and not every ghost is horrific. Buildings do not need a tragedy to become haunted...only a high emotional attachment. The love that one feels for an ancestral home may be enough for the spirit to linger, and welcome others to discover the joy that has kept that soul tethered to the physical world. Such places transcend labels such as "hotel" or "bed and breakfast,"

Carrington's Bluff

and remain more than a place to stay. They make the guest feel like more than a guest. They feel at home.

In looking for a Bed and Breakfast, many take location into consideration. Is it on a Main Street, easy to find, and near all the things a guest could want? For those looking for a location that is off the main drive, yet still near enough to the beauty of Austin, Carrington's Bluff may be just the place.

Its History

More than 120 years old, the home that is now Carrington Bluff's Bed and Breakfast began in 1877 as the Carrington Dairy Farm. It was one of the first homesteads of the Republic of Texas and has, in fact, stayed in the Carrington family for its entire existence. It operated as a dairy farm from its construction until the mid 1950s, when it was taken over by the second owners, relatives of the Carrington family named Howell. Nearly thirty years later, in 1986, another Carrington descendent named Fullbrook took over possession of the house and turned Carrington's Dairy Farm into Carrington's Bed and Breakfast.

While entire generations of the Carrington family have lived in the house, it should be noted that none of them are known to have died violent or untimely deaths. In fact, the home seems picture perfect... save for the reports of some of the guests.

Its Ghosts

From the guest books in every room, one can paint an interesting picture of the beautiful main house and writer's cottage. And while there have been no reports of malevolence or angry voices, it is clear that not everyone at Carrington's Bluff is a temporary guest.

One guest, a regular who's been staying there for around ten years, informed the manager that the television continuously clicked on and off throughout the night, though there was no remote control and no reasonable explanation. The manager looked back through the guest books and discovered that the regular was not the only one who'd had experiences with the "malfunctioning" television. Others observed similar phenomena over the years, and marked it dutifully in the guest book.

The manager has also experienced a few strange things, though she is reluctant to assign blame to otherworldly powers. In the kitchen, she reports, the lids from several containers have inexplicably popped off in front of her. Also, the chairs on the front porch, after having been arranged, have been moved toward the center of the porch by unseen hands.

Guests often told stories about a painting of two little girls in one of the rooms. Whether it was the power of suggestion or not, the guests claimed the eyes *followed* them when they walked past the painting. By coincidence, the painting hung in the same room where most reports of the paranormal are made. The manager moved the painting to another room and has never had another problem with it.

In addition, many guests claim to have seen "her," a middle-aged motherly type with long dark hair, walking the grounds and even in their rooms. She is not threatening, they insist, merely startling in her presence—and in her ability to disappear when seen. Who the woman is remains a mystery, but the common belief is that she is none other than Martha Hill Carrington, still strolling around her beloved home.

Perhaps the most interesting report came from a guest who claimed to feel the presence of the woman in her room. She was in the shower, she explained, when she felt hands massaging her scalp and washing her hair.

Present Day

Carrington's Bluff welcomes travelers for both business and leisure, and offers packages with specialties in mind. The main house has five lavishly furnished bedrooms, while the "Writer's Cottage" holds an additional three. They offer a wide range of amenities to ensure the comfort of their guests, including an enormous buffet style breakfast and Texas wine in the rooms. Though there have been no new reports over the last couple of years, management hasn't asked. Instead, they rely on the guest books in each room to document the good, bad, and strange points of the guests' time at Carrington's Bluff. And, while there doesn't seem to be a best time per se, most of the paranormal activity seems to stem from a single room in the house, the Martha Hill Carrington Room. Guests are encouraged to make reservations, especially if a specific room is desired, although walk-ups are welcome.

†††††

For reservations call toll-free,
1-888-290-6090.
For more information about Carrington's
Bluff, visit their website at www.
carringtonsbluff.com.

Inn at Pearl Street

809 West Martin Luther King Jr. Boulevard

M any people come to Austin every year on the most romantic of occasions—their honeymoon. The allure of the city is undeniable, with live music every night, fine restaurants, and scenic Town Lake just moments away from any location. But during such times, travelers may not want the same faceless hotels and generic rooms. They may wish for a break from the hustle and bustle of the inner city and seek a place that is a refuge of beauty and romance. Nestled on Pearl Street sits just a place, beautiful and quiet in every regard. Such is the beauty that some guests, it seems, decided to stay around long after their bodies checked out...not only from the hotel, but also from this plane of existence.

Bed and Breakfasts are unique for travelers, as they provide all the comforts of staying not in a hotel but a home. Most often operated out of historic buildings, these paragons of hospitality sometimes provide visitors with just a bit more than they'd bargained for. Not only are the beds comfortable and the food excellent, but the nighttime hallways sometimes see others that cannot be truly called guests...as they've been there longer than even the current owners—and will probably be there for as long as the building exists.

Inn at Pearl Street

Its History

At over 150 years old, the Inn at Pearl Street buildings are among the oldest in the "Uptown Cultural District of Judge's Hill." Built in 1896, the home's owner prior to 1914 is unknown; however, according to the city directory for that year, it belonged to a judge named Wilcox. Along with his wife, Stella Snider, and their five children, Wilcox enjoyed many years at the mansion and a few that were marred by tragedy. Of their five children, only three, all daughters, survived to adulthood. Wilcox's two sons died a few years apart. Both were two years old at the time of their deaths, and local legend has it that the boys both died on Easter Sunday.

Their three daughters never married, continuing to live together in the old house until their respective deaths.

During its life, the old home became the set of the movie "Slackers," as well as a co-op run by people described in much the same way.

During the 1980s, it hosted dance parties that were reported to be legendary in the amount of debauchery displayed. By the time it closed its doors again, the house was a neglected shell of its former beauty, waiting for the wrecking ball and developers to remove it from the street. In a stroke of good fortune, the house was bought and renovated and turned into the luxurious bed and breakfast that it is today. Even before it opened its doors, however, it was clear that there was more to this old house than met the eye at first glance.

The Ghosts

The first sign that all was not right with the old house came during renovation. According to several published reports, before the building had actually been wired for power, there were several occasions at night, when passersby, as well as the owner, saw the interior lights flashing on and off, and some even claimed to hear music coming from within.

The most common sighting, however, is also the most tragic. There have been several guests who've seen an old woman carrying a sick baby from room to room inside one of the buildings. She has also been sighted rocking the crying child in a chair that moves, whether she can be seen or not. The old woman is believed to be Stella Snider, still caring for one, or both, of her dead boys.

There are also reports of a second apparition, this one of a tall thin elderly man, who frequents the carriage house behind the main inn.

Present Day

The Inn at Pearl Street overcame its history long ago, transforming from a neglected building to a world-class establishment that was officially selected as Austin's only "Designer Showhouse." It was also voted the "Most Romantic Inn in Austin." The inn accepts reservations for both short-term and extended stays in any of their ten guestrooms, each decorated in their own distinct style. They serve breakfast every day, with mimosas on Sundays. As for Stella Snider, her apparition is still reported, as are cold spots and the occasional flickering lights. The old man appears less frequently, but occasionally still lets his presence be known.

To fully enjoy a Bed and Breakfast of the Inn at Pearl Street's caliber, one need only stay a few nights in their lap of comfort. Though many guests have reported seeing the old woman and her sickly baby, she seems to add more of a sense of charm than foreboding to the place. It seems, therefore, that the best time to visit the inn is when the romantic urge takes hold of one's heart.

††††††

For reservations, call 1-800-494-2203,
or visit their web site at
http://www.innpearl.com.

3

Haunted Bars and Restaurants

No matter where a person goes, every place has something to set it apart from any other place in the world. New Orleans is famous for it, as is Los Angeles. While some look to the architecture or the climate as the thing that sets it apart, the real divider is a place's individual *flavor*—and Austin has flavors a-plenty for hungry folks. From traditional Mexican food to Thai cuisine, nearly every culture is represented through food. Whether having breakfast, a light lunch, or even a full dinner, there is a flavor to satisfy even the most persnickety connoisseur.

After hours, the nightlife is just as exciting. Clubs of every kind invite guests in, tempting the ears with every kind of music, and the palate with the kinds of drinks that many have never even heard of. But while the music may be modern, pumped through twenty-first-century speakers, something older lurks near the bar. It isn't men going through a mid-life crisis looking for young girls, though those do exist in abundance. What lurks came even before them or their parents—and gives a whole new meaning to the word "retro." In Austin's bars and clubs, everyone can get their favorite spirits. But not every "spirit" comes in a bottle.

Speakeasy

412D Congress Avenue

E very building has a history, even those that are relatively new. When tragedy strikes, it is not uncommon for the new businesses to use pieces of a former business in construction, sometimes as a reminder of times past. Other times, a souvenir is claimed to remind patrons of the historical significance of the place that came before or as a reminder of good times. But when those items are attached to a tragedy, keeping such a totem may give the new owner a little more than they bargained for.

Austin has always been famous for its nightlife. From the days of "Guy Town" to the present, there has never been a shortage of entertainment in the city. When asking about places to go that have that "Austin" flavor, it's easy to get lost in the large-scale restaurants and bars. However, those unique places do exist. One just has to know where to look. And while out-of-the-way places do have their own flavor, some provide more entertainment than was bargained for, in the form of apparitions and patrons that stay long after closing...and refuse to leave when the doors are locked.

Its History

The building that houses "Speakeasy," the bar, is relatively new, only dating back around ninety years, yet it blends seamlessly with the buildings around it. Before it was built, there stood another building. Long rumored to be one of the fabled "speakeasies" of prohibition times,

Speakeasy

the building was actually a furniture shop owned by William Kreisle and his wife. They sold the building in 1899 to the Southwestern Telephone and Telegraph Company, and it remained in the company's possession for many years. Still, rumors abounded about the "real" nature of the building, as there was an entrance in an alley behind Congress Avenue. Rumors abounded about patrons, just like in the movies, having to whisper passwords through a sliding panel to gain entrance. An owl, it was said, behind the bar designated it as the place to be, a tradition that still holds with the current owners.

In July 1916, tragedy struck when the building caught fire and burned to the ground. While the fire raged, a brave fireman rushed inside, attempting to rescue two women. The three became trapped in the inferno and lost their lives, seeking shelter inside a metal elevator.

For a long while after the building was rebuilt, there were reports of strange occurrences, but no attention was paid. When the building was purchased and reopened as a bar, the activity began again with vigor.

The Ghosts

The souls from that fateful blaze in 1916 still appear to be trapped in the building, though the brick and mortar have changed. There exists in the main room a closet, the walls of which were part of the original building. The former owners used to staple flowers to the ceiling and tape them to the walls to keep the restless souls appeased. After hearing what they described as screams and cries when the old flowers were removed, the new owners decided to replace the old flowers and add new ones of their own. The screaming, they say, stopped.

The front doors bang when unattended by anyone, followed by the sounds of hurried feet rushing up the stairs. And patrons and employees alike have also reported screams. There have been several investigations of the site, many of which claim that the stairwell is the second most haunted spot in the building.

The most haunted spot, however, hangs over the main stage, where apparitions have been sighted around and in it for quite some time. It is, in fact, the now antique elevator that ran in the original building... and in which two women and a fireman lost their lives. Several have glanced up during the course of the night's festivities, only to have a chill run up their spine as they see the plaintive face of a woman staring out the open doors at them. Many times, patrons have reported seeing two women and a man standing in the old iron box, as if attending the club in their own private seating.

Present Day

Speakeasy is now a famous club in Austin, due in no small part to its otherworldly patrons. It's comprised of three levels, including a rooftop terrace, and is furnished in the style of the roaring twenties. Live music plays nightly, and patrons can indulge in a romantic candlelit dinner as well as dancing. From the rooftop, one can see the breathtaking Austin skyline. And while the bright neon sign may be clearly visible, true to the name, the main entrance can be a bit of a trick to find. Yes, it's in an alley, though you don't need a password to get in.

Both patrons and employees have reported seeing the faces in the elevator—whether the bar is open for business or not. However, it's during the month of July that sightings increase, near the anniversary of the fatal blaze. When visiting, one never knows who might be watching your table.

✝✝✝✝✝

To find out more about Speakeasy, visit their website at http://www.speakeasyaustin.com/, or call 512-477-2789 to book a party.

The Tavern

Corner of 12th Street and Lamar Avenue

t sits on the corner of a busy thoroughfare, a strange anachronism against the modern backdrop. It is, after all, downtown Austin and the twenty-first century, and the small German-style cottage stands out amid the concrete shops and shining pavement. One gets the impression that it has been there, forgotten, since such buildings were in fashion, and one would not be far from correct. While it has stood for the better part of ninety

The Tavern

years, it has never been forgotten. And inside, there are things, it seems, that will always be reminders of its place in Austin's history and lore.

All across the city are theme restaurants and bars, places that have taken an existing building and remodeled it to resemble, for example, an Irish pub, or have a film-noir theme. Bars and restaurants come and go in Austin with such frequency that some only stay open for a month or two before changing hands. While, at first glance, the Tavern may seem like one of the many, it has actually been there longer than most and has seen its share of times both good and bad.

Its History

In what may be called either a miscalculation or a blunder, depending upon who is asked, the Tavern got off to a rocky start. Constructed in 1921, the building was the dream of Niles Graham, who wanted nothing more than to open a German pub on what was then a dirt road. However, a new law, called Prohibition, came into effect and dashed his hopes of the pub to bits.

With the building completed, but unable to sell alcohol, Graham leased the building out for the next twelve years as Enfield Grocery. Rumor has it that during this time, Graham, undeterred by silly things like laws, used the grocery store as a front, out of which he ran a brothel and speakeasy. During the Great Depression, the grocery store moved next door, allowing Graham to realize his dream, first as a restaurant and then as the bar he'd always wanted. It has stayed in operation as a restaurant and bar ever since.

The Ghosts

Though the nature of Graham's operations can only be defined as rumor, there is no way to determine just who haunts the Tavern. But there can be no doubt that the place is haunted. Many have seen the ghost, named "Emily" by the staff, as well as her daughter.

According to lore, at some point when the building was in operation as a brothel, a fight broke out. A young prostitute named Emily, as well as her daughter, were caught up in the middle of the fracas and were killed.

Emily is the most often sighted apparition, commonly seen climbing the stairs, walking into the kitchen, or just walking past the bar. She's also been seen standing next to the pool table and sitting by the door. On every occasion, she appears the same, with short hair and wearing a dress from the 1920s or 30s. Her daughter is also seen, most commonly sitting on a second-floor window ledge.

Emily is also thought to be behind other strange phenomena, such as glasses flying off the walls on the first and second floors, tapping and pinching the waitstaff, and also for changing the television channels to something more ladylike than sports stations. Employees have also heard footsteps from the upstairs floor when it was empty, as well as the sounds of someone engaged in a round of billiards when there is no one in the room.

Emily was also once spotted from across the street by a fellow working at a gas station. He glanced up and saw her standing in the second floor window, staring down at him. While seeing visitors in the Tavern is not uncommon, the place was not yet open for business when she was seen...and she *disappeared* in the blink of an eye.

Present Day

Still in operation, the Tavern is a popular spot for not only drinks, but also for its food. The upper rooms still bear the numbers that it had when the place offered more than groceries or alcohol. Paranormal enthusiasts have investigated it several times—and they've all come away with the conclusion that the place is indeed haunted and that the ghosts are still very active.

Though most phenomena seem to happen when the bar is not open to business, customers often talk about walking into a chilly breeze just after seeing the hazy outline of a woman. According to some sources, however, ordering the chicken-fried steak is a sure way to get the woman's attention, as it is one of her favorites.

†††††

To find out more about the Tavern, such as their daily specials, one need only visit their website at http://www.austintavern.com, or call them at 512-320-8377.

Buffalo Billiards

201 East 6th Street

Not every haunted house has high peaks and looming windows. They're not filled with cobwebs and moon-faced servants with hollow eyes and cackling laughter. Some, in fact, are where folks least expect to find them and the things that go bump in the night are by design—and the shadows are there by purpose. Wherever there might have been tragedy, wherever emotions run high...there exists the potential for a haunting. And no matter what occupies the space in the physical world, the restless souls will continue to walk from the world beyond.

Buffalo Billiards

Across the street from the Driskill Hotel, one can find any type of entertainment. There are coffee shops, bars, and shopping within easy walking distance. On the opposite side of 6th Street sits an old building, and from it comes the sounds of clacks and voices. The sounds are not otherworldly, for the place is a pool hall called Buffalo Billiards, but it is *after* the doors close around two o'clock in the morning that strange things happen—and the dead decide to shoot a game or two.

Its History

The building at 201 East 6th Street began over 140 years ago as the first boarding house in old Austin. Named the "Missouri House," it was built and run by the Ziller family. While there is no proof, rumor has it that there was more going on in their bedrooms than just boarding. The house, it seems, also operated as a brothel. Whether true or not, what can be verified is the fact that, since its construction, the Missouri House has served the city of Austin and its citizens in various ways. After it closed as a boarding house, it was reopened as a bar and then a store, and has been home for a string of other businesses. Regardless of the trade going on under its roof, the Missouri House remained a community place to meet and discuss business.

When the Driskill Hotel was built across the street, it continued to serve the city and the Driskill's guests as a bar.

Over the years, the building has received a facelift or two, and now houses Buffalo Billiards, a popular pool hall. It didn't take long, however, for the new owner to discover that some of his patrons refused to leave, and not everything with his business venture was as it should be.

The Ghosts

Within a week of opening, the manager of Buffalo Billiards called the police about strange goings-on. The previous night, he'd followed his routine of returning all the pool cues to the racks and the balls to their cases. He set the alarm and locked the doors behind him as he went. The next morning, he returned to find every pool cue lying on tables, as if someone had just finished playing a round. Even more, the balls were all out of their cases and several were on the floor. When the police arrived, they scoured the building, but could find no trace of a break-in, or any living thing inside the building. The doors were still locked when the manager arrived, and the alarm code was still active.

Occurrences are not limited to the bottom floor. The upper story, known as the "Orbit Lounge," has had its share of strange phenomena. One story involves a woman who was mopping up at the end of the day. As she cleaned, she had the feeling of someone watching her—and became anxious to get out of the place quickly. When she was finished, she shut off the lights...and then felt someone tap her on the shoulder. She turned, but saw nothing but the darkened room behind her. The woman quit her job and never returned.

While the identities of the restless souls in the building are unknown, one can assume they come from the time when the Missouri building welcomed all guests and likely saw its fair share of tragedy.

Present Day

Buffalo Billiards and the Orbit Lounge are open daily from 4 p.m. until 2 a.m. The building is easy to find, and the staff is helpful, but there are still some who swear they can *feel* eyes on them as they work or shoot a game and it's not uncommon to step into a chill.

Stay until closing and play a few rounds. Have a good time, but as with any haunting, strange things can happen at unexpected times. The playful spooks of the old building do not seem to adhere to any set schedule, but they do most their work when the doors are locked. There are large windows at the front of the building, where one can watch for any strangeness, but eyes must be kept sharp. If you blink, you might miss it.

†††††

For more information about Buffalo Billiards, visit their web site at http://www. buffalobilliards.com/austin. To arrange a private party, one can call 512-479-7665.

The Jacoby-Pope Building

(Logan's on 6th Street)

200 East 6th Street

Sixth Street tends to glow after dark—the neon from shops and bars casting strange colors on the street and passersby. It beats with a pulse of its own, partly from the music playing within the bars, partly from those who frequent the nightspots. Still, there is another beat that courses under the city's streets and buildings. Taking a seat inside a dark lounge or tavern, one can feel the heart of the city beating in its own time. Its breath is a cold wind that springs from nowhere, its presence felt by clinking glasses. This pulse continues even after the bands have stopped, as the phantom heartbeats of those whose hearts beat no more can still be heard.

Walking down 6th Street, visitors are quickly awed by the grand Driskill, the high Littlefield Building, and the massive Capitol. But there are other, less assuming places in which history is never forgotten—nor is it at rest. Ghosts don't only come from murder, but from accidental tragedy as well.

Its History

The building at 200 East 6th Street may seem like a modern building, but in truth it was built before the turn of the twentieth century. Built in 1874, it is quite plain when compared to its extravagant neighbor, the Hannig building. However, it was not designed to be extravagant. It was built by a gentleman named Jacoby, who apparently never used

That Jacoby-Pope Building (Logan's on 6th Street)

the place. Intended, perhaps, as a storefront, the building became little more than a small storage house for a while.

It did, however, become useful, as citizens began to hold wine-tastings and other such functions there. In fact, the place became well known for the spirits within its walls long before anyone spoke of a haunting.

Over the years, the building has changed hands many times, holding various businesses. It has been several bars, storefronts, even a coffee shop. During the time when it was reputedly a coffee storehouse and refinery, tragedy occurred. According to legend, a worker fell into the hopper of the coffee grinder. The results were most horrid, driving the business to close its doors. While there is no concrete evidence of such an event, it would explain some of the reported phenomena in the building.

Late in the twentieth century, the Jacoby-Pope building seemed to come full circle, as it again turned into a bar—and once again became famous for the spirits within.

The Ghosts

Whether or not the story of the fallen coffee-plant worker is true, there is something that lurks behind the bar on East 6th Street. Though none have seen the spirit, his presence has been felt nonetheless.

The most common phenomena reported inside the bar includes glassware that swings in racks unaided by living hands. Some patrons sit in the bar staring, their train of thought lost as the glasses clink together, though there is no one near them and they have not been bumped.

Glasses are not the only things that move in the bar. Doors also have been reported to swing, as if pushed by someone coming in or going out of the bar. When checked, there is no one there, and the doors hang peacefully closed until the next disturbance.

The most unnerving phenomenon usually occurs once the bar is closed and the building supposedly empty. Loud cracking sounds—as if billiard balls are striking each other—are often heard from the second floor. Upon investigation, there is nothing broken, nor is there anyone in the upstairs rooms.

Some patrons also talk of cold gusts of air in the summer, and the strange sense that they are being watched...even when their backs are *against* the wall.

Present Day

Asking locals where to find the Jacoby-Pope building may draw blank stares and head-scratches, but most know the bar that sits there now. Logan's on 6th Street is a popular bar on the main strip. And while most go in looking for spirits of a different kind, those that work there know about the phenomena that still occurs today. Far from being afraid, though, they tend to just accept their permanent patrons as a part of everyday life in the bar.

Though there is no schedule kept of when the ghost of Logan's makes himself known, most of the activity takes place just before closing time or soon thereafter. It stands to reason, then, that the best time to go to Logan's is whenever one desires a drink. Those wanting to experience the haunting, however, need only stay late, tip well, and keep their eyes on the glasses hanging over the bar.

††††††

For more information about this unique bar,
call 512-236-0300.

4
Haunted Theaters

There aren't too many places where shadows are intentional. Even in a place like Austin, most people turn away from the unusual, darkened rooms where disembodied voices from the past speak and images of the long dead can still be seen. There are, however, a few places where many go to sit in a darkened room while shadows play against a wall and the voices speak of love and terror. We call them theaters. While there are quite a few in Austin, both film and live, there are only a precious handful in which there needs be no audience, no projector, and no actors. The voices still come out of the dark without the benefit of flesh or film, but these are not the voices of Bogart and Hepburn...*they are the voices of the dead*.

Every theater seems to have a "patron ghost," a guiding spirit to ensure a good show and watch over the actors. While some call it superstition, others call it tradition. Still others, however, call the ghosts real. In Austin, the performance on stage may just take a back seat to what's happening behind the back row, what's pushing the curtains, or who may be watching from an empty box seat.

The Paramount Theater

713 Congress Avenue

Stepping through the doors is a step into another time long past. Before the days of multi-screen theaters, there stood show palaces of such magnitude that going to the theater was a real event. Below the high domed ceiling, the seats are comfortable and the carpets soft. The walls are carved and painted with remarkable beauty. It's easy to forget the year, especially when there are so many reminders of the past... the gentleman, for example, puffing his cigar in the balcony, or the feeling that even up higher, over the stage, someone watches the audience. Perhaps it is the spirits of the theater—*the ghosts of performances past*—that thicken the air and whisper in the dark. Or perhaps there is something more in the highest seats, down the dark corridors, and behind the curtains.

In what part of a building lies its soul? Is it in the brick and mortar? Or perhaps it's the furniture and fabrics that make up its trappings? More likely, the soul of any building rests with those who walked its halls, who gave their best within its walls, and who made that building a special place and gave it a legacy. In some cases, such a soul is not content to simply sit and bask in former glory. Its past is a living thing that cannot be ignored, even if parts of that past came before the building itself.

The Paramount Theater

Its History

The Paramount Theater first opened its doors to patrons in 1915, a giant of a showplace built by Ernest Nalle. The lot on which it stands, however, was used since the days of the Republic of Texas. Where now stands the main auditorium once sat three log structures, the original offices of the Republic's Department of War. A hotel also stood on the site, but it too was lost to time and progress. When Nalle began to build his theater, it was March 1915. Only eight months later, and at a cost of nearly $150,000, the theater, then called the Majestic, began its legacy.

During the first fourteen years of its existence, the Majestic played host to all the greats of Vaudeville. For each performance, the house was packed with patrons listening to the songs and jokes of the Marx Brothers, fantastic rope tricks of Will Rogers, and even the mystifying prowess of Harry Houdini. However, the demise of Vaudeville signaled a change for the theater, with first silent and then talking pictures.

In 1929, the Majestic was bought by Carl Hoblitzelle, who remodeled the theater to fit with more modern times. He renamed it the Paramount—and a second era was born. Still catering to both live theater and movies, the Paramount featured ballet, afternoon mysteries, and live music from the likes of John Phillip Sousa. Live theater, however, was falling out of fashion in favor of movies, and by the 1950s, the theater showed almost exclusively films. Still, another modernization very nearly signaled the end for the Paramount: television.

Credit for rescuing the Paramount from the wrecking ball rests squarely with a trio of businessmen, John Bernardoni, Charles Echerman, and Stephen Scott. Bernardoni thought that such a theater should not go to waste, and wanted to bring back live theater to Austin. Despite naysayers and downtown's bad reputation, the three of them persevered and opened the Paramount's first live performance since anyone could remember in 1975. Two years later, the theater began a massive restoration, which lasted until 1980.

The Ghosts

Whether they are the souls of past performances or the restless dead, the Paramount Theater breathes. Behind her heavy curtain and beneath her domed ceiling, patrons can *feel* the past watching...and sometimes the past pops up to say hello. Here is a listing of the alleged haunts.

† The first ghost to make his presence known has never been positively identified. He sits in the balcony area, his presence heralded by the heavy scent of cigar smoke. Those who have seen him describe him as wearing attire from when the theater first opened—more than ninety years ago. Neither malicious nor benevolent, he simply sits, as if waiting for the next performance to begin.

† Another apparition sighted is that of a woman, though her identity is also unknown. Tony Johnson, the head custodian for twenty-five years, remembered seeing her one day while vacuuming the carpets in the lobby. She came down the stairs, turned the corner, and made her way toward the ladies restroom. However, the door she went in led only to Johnson's closet. He followed, close behind, but when he opened his door...the woman was gone. It should also be noted that the only other person in the theater at that time, his assistant, was upstairs cleaning the balcony and could not have been the woman he sighted.

† Several people have reported a curious sensation of being watched, or of presences directly behind them. The most common area for such phenomena is in the upper section of the balcony, which, years ago, was the only area in which blacks were allowed to sit. The old "Coloreds Only" box office still remains, the entrance for which sits in an alley. Johnson once attempted to make the old ticket booth his office, only to abandon the project because of the bad feelings that accompanied the room.

† The projection booth also has a curious history, leaving many to believe it, too, is haunted. Two projectionists have died in the booth. The first passed away due to unknown circumstances. The second suffered a heart attack during the second reel of Casablanca in 2000.

† The most haunted room in the Paramount, however, is not the projection booth, nor is it the old ticket window. It is a small bathroom behind the projectionist's booth. Unchanged since 1915, the narrow bathroom is walled with rough-hewn brick and mortar, and it is in this bathroom that the voices of a man and woman can be plainly heard, though their conversation has yet to be deciphered. While some have theorized that the voices are actually just sounds of whatever movie is playing bleeding through the walls, most reports come while no film is running.

Present Day

Now fully restored, Paramount Theater is a testament to a forgotten age when theaters were show palaces, before the birth of the megaplex. For all the modernizations, there are still echoes of the past throughout the building. The domed ceiling, for instance, is a lavishly painted portrait, looking down on the audience. The boxes, stage left and right, are brilliantly ornate in design. And, hanging over the stage, is the original fire-curtain from 1915, discovered during the 1975 renovation, hand painted and beautiful. There are even places where the foundation of the Department of War buildings can be seen, if one knows where to look. And, for those who know where to look, there is still a hole in the ceiling, above which sits a block and tackle placed there by none other than Harry Houdini. Still a fine example of extravagance and class, it hosts Hollywood movie premieres, live theater, dance performances, and classic movies.

The list of greats who have performed on Paramount's stage has also grown. Martha Graham, Paul Taylor, and Merce Cunningham have all had their companies perform for Austin on her stage. Lily Tomlin and the late George Carlin have made Austin laugh within her walls. Even Tibetan Monks have chanted on the main stage.

But what of those patrons and performers who simply refuse to leave? They're still there, says Tony Johnson, and as active as ever.

Sitting in the audience at the Paramount, it is hard to imagine a bad time to visit. Even in an empty house, the Paramount is a sight to behold. Still, to fully appreciate the old building, one needs simply to buy a ticket. To encounter those that do not rest, however, the best advice is similar. Employees and patrons have sighted them at all times of the day. When visiting Paramount, keep vigilant, because they appear without warning, and you never know who might be sitting next to you.

††††††

To find out what's playing, whether live performances or movies, at either the Paramount or its sister, the State Theater, visit their website at http://www.austintheatre.org, or call 512-472-5470.

The Hideout

617 Congress Avenue

There are places in Austin where darkened rooms are the norm, where dozens go to enjoy the spectacle, and where some stand in breathless anticipation because they don't know what's going to happen. Surely not unique in the world, these places are few in Austin, as they provide a form of entertainment of the most unpredictable nature. These places are the homes of improvisational troupes, performers who have a great deal of talent, and no script. And just when the audience thinks the show is over, there are other things that occur outside the confines of the stages that let them know that here, anything can—and often does—happen.

Most actors are, by their own admission, a superstitious lot. Pre-show rituals, the customary "break a leg" instead of "good luck," and the refusal to quote anything from "Macbeth" within the theater are only a few curiosities in theater lore. Another commonly accepted notion is that every theater has at least one ghost. Whether real or imagined, almost every theater has some sort of "patron spirit" that looks down on the performers and ensures a good show. In some cases, the "ghost" is nothing more than an idolized actress who may never have set foot in the theater. In other cases, the spirits are very real. At the Hideout, however, there is no doubt...as its ghost has been making himself known for years.

The Hideout

Its History

The building that sits at 617 Congress Avenue is unassuming. It's a two-story storefront that, up until a few years ago, stood empty and waiting for the right business to come along. However, according to Austin's historical societies, the building has been around almost since Austin was declared the state capitol.

Built in 1849 by a gentleman named Wahrenberger, the lot was a gift from the city for Wahrenberger's part in thwarting a plot to move the state capitol back to Houston. The building became the city's first bakery and general store. In 1862, the building became the Kluge Restaurant and Saloon, and stayed in business until 1880. Mr. Kluge met with a tragic and curiously untimely demise while bathing in Shoal Creek, where he drowned in less than three feet of water. Though the circumstances surrounding his drowning were suspicious, no arrests were ever made, and the building again changed hands.

During its life, the old storefront has been used as a saloon, a dry cleaning shop, a men's clothing store, and a dozen other businesses, all of which had difficulty staying open due to the rapidly changing economy in Austin. Prior to the 1990s, it was a pawnshop, a shoe store, and even a billiards hall. When it closed its doors, the building stood vacant for years until it was purchased and renovated by the current owners, Sean Hill and Shana Merlin, and was reborn as the Hideout.

During renovation, the owners found many remnants of the past businesses that once occupied the space, including liver spot oil bottles and old newspapers. The renovations also seemed to stir up more than dust and history. They discovered that, though vacant, the building was not completely uninhabited.

The Ghosts

Though no one is really sure exactly who is haunting the building, most assume it's Mr. Kluge who walks the halls, and it does seem clear that he has a sense of humor. Or perhaps he's just trying to blend in with the performers. Either way, he fits right in with the rest of the cast. The first clue of otherworldly inhabitance came during the renovation, when a breaker tripped for no apparent reason. A subsequent wiring check provided no clues or reasons, but it was far from the last prank played by whatever—or whomever—still resides within. Workers also noted several unexplained problems with the plumbing, including faucets that turned on when a plumber was trying to install new pipes.

Performers have reported gates that lock and unlock themselves, as well as faucets that turn themselves on and off. While playful, and sometimes unnerving, the spirit has never seemed malevolent in any way. Some call it the overactive imaginations of some talented performers, but it may just be the troop's resident guardian making his presence known.

Present Day

The Hideout is a thriving business that provides Austin with improvisational comedy, courtesy of their resident troop, the Heroes of Comedy, as well as independent film and live music and theater. The building's first floor holds a fifty-seat coffee house and cabaret stage, while the second floor houses the seventy-four seat black-box theater. The theaters are also used as classrooms for courses in improvisational comedy with beginning to advanced levels. In addition, the coffee house provides another service—it is the meeting place for the beginning of a ninety-minute walking tour of downtown Austin, courtesy of Austin Ghost Tours.

While the guardian spirit of the theater may not appear, his presence can always be felt, and performers often speak fondly of their own experiences with their resident phantom. The absolute best time to visit, though, is when the visitor needs a cup of great coffee, or feels the need to laugh.

†††††

To check the Hideout's schedule, visit its website at http://www.hideouttheater.com. The ghost tours follow a different schedule, which can be obtained from the Hideout's box office.

4

Haunted Schools

Often times I'm asked, "What causes a haunting?" I wish there was an easy answer, a catchall formula that states with certainty what conditions have to come together to create a haunting. The trouble is, no one knows for certain. Tragic deaths, for one, seems to be a large cause, but there are too many people who've died and are *not* still poking around for anyone to name it as a definitive cause. Unfinished business is another phrase heard around spiritualists and paranormal enthusiasts. A third type of haunting seems to replay over and over again, a *loop frozen in time* that does not react to people or objects around them. The only binding thread between them all seems to be powerful emotions. Places where emotions run high, such as hospitals, churches, and even airports, tend to have the odds in their favor of being haunted by an entity or two. Small wonder, then, that every school has a story.

Institutes of higher learning are breeding grounds of new ideas, colliding hormones, and emotional instability. It's part of the process of growing up that children experience new feelings and know neither what they mean nor how to control them. Whether it's the onset of puberty or the pangs of young love, those emotions are never more intense than during school days—and those feelings leave traces. Imprints left behind give a school its history, its pride. And sometimes...those who came before refuse to leave the halls of their alma mater.

Metz Elementary School

84 Robert T. Martinez Jr. Street

The hallways are filled with children, the scent of chalk, and textbooks. Happy shouts accompany the bells that signal the end of the day, when a sea of youth surges toward the door, washing its way down the sidewalk on the way to busses and homes. The doors lock, and as the last of the faculty walks away, he turns, casting a furtive glance down the darkened hallway. Are there pranksters lurking in the halls, waiting for after school mischief, or only memories of days gone

Metz Elementary School

by, when the quiet elementary school once captured the attention of the world for events both curious and chilling? Perhaps it is a little of both, but for now, at least, the hallways are quiet again.

There are a few consistencies where hauntings are concerned. Their reasons are as varied as the lives that came before them. In some cases, a horrific death can be the cause. In others, unfinished business prompts the soul to remain long after the body has passed over. But in *every* case, there are high emotions that mark the trappings of the haunted location. For some, that emotion is hate. For others, love. In the case of Metz Elementary, however, the emotions could be simply defined as "school spirit."

Its History

The Metz Elementary that stands today is a new structure, designed with modern conveniences and a testament to architectural functionality and grace. However, the building is young, and inherited the name from the near-legendary building that stood on the same grounds years before.

First opened in 1916, the original Metz Elementary was mired in controversy. That same year, the Austin school board ruled that children who spoke primarily Spanish would attend a school apart from those who spoke primarily English. Their opinion was that the Spanish-speaking children could more effectively learn if they were taught in a mixture of Spanish and English. The Mexican-American community took umbrage, however, seeing the measure as a form of segregation. Coupled with the fact that the school to which their children would be shipped was several miles away, making attendance difficult for some and impossible for others, the Mexican-American community protested. Though the board never admitted their mistake or that their plan was merely thinly-veiled racism and an attempt at segregation, they quietly backed down, and the Spanish-speaking children were allowed to stay at Metz Elementary.

For more than seventy years, Metz Elementary served the community, providing a legacy of learning that endured until 1989, when the neighborhood outgrew the school. The school board voted to tear down the old building to make way for a new one that could better accommodate the growing community and increased enrollment.

The building stood empty for several years while plans were drawn up for demolition. By the time crews arrived, vandals had invaded the building and left their mark. Graffiti covered the walls where lunch menus once hung, lockers were pulled from their resting places, and many of the windows were broken out. The building held an ominous air, but none of the city workers were prepared for the events that followed.

The first reports came on the first day from several workers who claimed to hear the laughter of children echoing through the supposedly empty building. Though the old school was searched, no trace of the children was found. However, stranger events began to shake the city workers, many of which revolved around writing that appeared on previously empty chalkboards. Several pieces of well-maintained equipment stopped functioning without reason. As bulldozers approached the walls, the engines stalled out. Even the workmen themselves were not immune from the strange activity, as their watches would stop as they approached the building.

Workmen began to quit, walking off the job in mid shift or simply not showing up at all. National newspapers picked up the story, especially when strange injuries began occurring on the site, all to the echoing sounds of children's laughter. Some workmen even reported looking up into the broken windows to find several pale faces staring down at him. When a falling wall killed a workman, the city took notice. Clergy was brought in to bless the land, and the demolition was finally able to continue.

The Ghosts

There are no records indicating deaths of any kind in the school, but that doesn't change the testimony of the workmen who swear that phantom children did not want to see their beloved school demolished. From the messages on the boards to the laughter, from accidents to broken equipment, those that worked on the demolition know that the haunting was real. But the real question that remains is to the cause. Was it the children who fought for their rights to learn that refused to leave, or was it something more macabre? And, although the original building is gone, will the spirits continue to haunt the new school that bears its name? Though the answers will likely never be known, there are those who feel that ghosts can never truly be silenced...and wait with dread for the laughter to begin again.

Present Day

The new school stands on the old grounds, bearing the name of its infamous predecessor. Once again, children roam the halls and laugh and shout as they learn the fundamentals of a bright future. The hallways after hours are, for now at least, quiet. Though the building looks nothing like the one that came before, the soul of the school is the same one of dedication and pride that prompted at least a few students to never leave.

Metz Elementary is a functioning school, and as such is not open for visitation. While it is clearly visible from the street, one must take care not to disturb or distract the students. The best time to visit, therefore, is when looking for a good education for a child. Just remember that at Metz Elementary, "school spirit" has an entirely different meaning than it may in any other school in Texas.

University of Texas, Austin Campus

F or 50,000 people, the University of Texas Austin campus on the "forty acres" is the center of their universe. It's a place to learn not only the skills needed to survive in the world, but also about who they are and what direction their lives will take. Rich in history, the school dates back to almost the very beginning of Austin, and has seen both greatness and tragedy in its students.

From humble beginnings, the plan for the college was formed in 1839, when the Congress of the Republic of Texas declared Austin the capitol and ordered a large parcel of land be set aside for higher education. It was not until 1883 that the first class of students took to the books, with a staff of only eight professors, four assistants, and one proctor. The students numbered only 221. Now, more than a century later, the campus boasts a history rich in folklore and legend. Some legends are innocuous, as how the campus mascot, a stuffed longhorn cow named BEVO, actually got its name. After a victory of 13-0 by longtime rivals Texas A&M, as the story goes, students branded the dismal score into the statue's side. To save face, the UT students altered the brand, giving the longhorn its name.

There are other legends, however, that give the campus a darker tint, where buildings echo with the screams of the past and where landmarks become grim reminders of tragedy. Still, the history is embraced, as it is part of what makes UT distinctive and allows it to hold its place as unique in Texas. And while stories of long-dead professors who haunt their former classrooms persist as urban legends, at least two have their roots in history, with enough sightings to earn those buildings the dubious moniker of "haunted."

University of Texas Tower

The Tower

It rises above the skyline, visible from almost any point in the city, a symbol of greatness of the institute of higher learning. Across its face is carved the words "Ye shall know the truth, and the truth shall make you free." But for some who remember, the tower stands as a reminder of darker times, when a single person captured the attention of the nation through his outpouring of madness and pain. And within the structure the past does not rest nor will it...until the people are given the proper chance to heal and mourn. Do whispers and screams still echo in the hallways, or is it just the past bleeding through to the present? On the campus of UT Austin, the Tower stands as both a symbol of strength and a reminder of pain.

When tragedy strikes, many times those affected by it do not wish to remember. So deep runs the pain that, for a time, the easiest thing to do is block it out. Yet, it's only when the tragedies of the past are marked instead of hidden that healing can begin—and a once proud monument can resume its former glory. Such a place exists for the students of the University of Texas, and though the pain of the past can still be heard, one can only hope that the cries grow quieter every year.

Its History

Completed in 1937, the main building featured a grand landmark, the likes of which had not before been seen in Texas. It rose 307 feet into the air, as there was a law in effect that stated that no building could be taller than the city's centerpiece, the Capitol building, which peaked at 311 feet. However, due to construction on a six-foot rise, the building actually wound up the tallest structure in Austin for quite some time.

Since the time of its opening, the Tower seemed to inspire not only awe, but darker thoughts for a few. It became a favorite spot for jumpers for the next forty years, racking up nine suicides by 1974.

The darkest chapter in the history of the tower, however, came on August 1, 1966, when a young architectural engineering student barricaded himself in the observation deck and unleashed hell on those below him. Charles Witman, a former marine, seemed to have a bright future. However, on July 31, he murdered his wife and mother. The next day, he climbed to the top of the Tower and opened fire on the students below, leaving fourteen dead and thirty-one wounded. The onslaught lasted for only ninety-three minutes, ending with a shot from a police officer that took Witman's life.

The Tower was closed for a time after the tragedy. Books and movies were written about what became referred to as one of the nation's first mass murders. When it did open again, it did not stay so for long. The ninth suicide in late 1974 closed the tower for more than twenty years.

The Ghosts

Perhaps it's just the knowledge of what happened on that awful day in August that haunts the building, but there have been reports of paranormal activity stemming from the deaths surrounding the Tower. Cold spots are reported in the stairwell, as well as feelings of foreboding and claustrophobia. It seems the closer some people get to the top of the Tower, the more intense and malignant the feelings become. While not everyone senses these emotions, the number who has is significant enough to warrant a second thought.

Those same people claim to hear quiet screaming and cries of anguish from outside the Tower, as if it were that day in 1966 and the killings were going on. Also heard are phantom gunshots and the barking of police officers who are trying to get into the building.

Present Day

After many years of being closed, the Tower was once again opened in 1999, but with a few precautions taken. No longer open, the Tower boasts iron rails and Plexiglas to discourage both jumpers and those who would follow Witman's example. By reopening, the Tower has been given back to the campus and students, and once again holds a place of honor on the landscape. It is now the site of marriage proposals, commencement ceremonies, and even public debates. During the week, the fifty-six bells of the Knicker Carillon ring on the hour from atop the structure. And while the great words are still visible across its face, so too are the bullet holes from so many years ago.

The Tower also holds an important place in the culture of the college, as one can tell how well the school is doing by how the Tower is lit. Bathed in orange with a "#1" signals when the school's president determines an extraordinary accomplishment, or when any varsity team has one an NCAA championship. Unbroken orange is the sign for commencement, although it is also lit this way for any victory over archrivals, Texas A&M. It is also lit this way for Texas Independence Day and July 4th. If only the top is orange, it is either Easter, Memorial Day, or UT sports has achieved victory in the Big XII. It is also lit similarly for Thanksgiving and Christmas. If, however, the top is lit in orange and white, it indicates either an NCAA or Big XII tie.

The campus is open to tours, and the Tower is accessible for a small fee to sightseers. However, if it is the more macabre experience people seek, most of the feelings and sounds are experienced on the first day of August every year. Lest we forget.

††††

The Littlefield Home

The Littlefield Home

Every town, no matter how large or small, has one. *That* house. It's the one that juts from the earth as though not built but born. At once horrifyingly out of place but beautiful in its design, *that* house earns the peculiar distinction of being the one whispered about. A campus so large that it is a city unto itself is no exception. While there are some who debate philosophy or what may come, this house still stands as the testament. It is the one about which freshmen are told stories to keep them in their dorms at night, for it has the curious distinction of being haunted.

Touring the UT Austin campus, one is taken aback by the immensity of the buildings in all their modern glory. While there are some places where architecture from a different time period creeps in, it is, for the most part, a campus full of monoliths and high buildings. Their very presence is a testament to modern learning, but on the south end of campus…there stands one glorious anomaly.

Its History

Built in 1893, the large Victorian mansion was the home of George Littlefield and his wife, Alice. During their lives at the house, it was only one of many, with an entire neighborhood of similarly extravagant homes claiming the space.

Littlefield, who built the tower of his namesake in downtown Austin, was a shrewd businessman, strong and outspoken, and filled with seemingly endless generosity. Among his endowments to the university was the Littlefield Fund for Southern History, an unheard-of $225,000 toward the purchase of the John Henry Wrenn Library, funds for the Littlefield Memorial Fountain, as well as the six statues that surround it. He also erected the Alice Littlefield Dormitory, and donated half a million dollars toward the construction of the campus' main building.

Yet, for all his generosity, there was another side to the happy Littlefield lifestyle. It is widely believed that, while away, Littlefield would lock his wife in the attic to avoid her being taken by Yankee soldiers who were unaware of the end of the Civil War. During her stays in the attic, she was assaulted mercilessly by bats, driving the poor woman slowly mad.

Alice Littlefield is often described as a manic-depressive whose melancholy states often lasted for days or even weeks. Her fear of the outside world bordered on agoraphobic, and she worried for her husband's safety while he was away. Some reports imply that she slowly lost her grip on sanity later in life.

When she died in 1935, the home was donated to the college, which allowed it to be saved when all the other houses of the neighborhood were demolished. Over the years, the house has been used in many different capacities, including the Austin and University of Texas Centennial Office and the Music Department. At one point, the Navy R.O.T.C. occupied the building, using the attic for a shooting range and mounting a cannon on the front lawn.

The Ghosts

While some point to the building's impressive architecture and Gothic arches as the reasoning behind the rumors of ghostly activity, those who have been in the building know that it does more than just look spooky. There is someone who still occupies the house... and her name is Alice Littlefield.

General feelings of uneasiness accompany the impression of being watched, making none of the employees want to be the first to arrive or the last to leave. Described as a sense of being trapped, several employees state that it's as if they will reach the doors and find that they won't open.

In addition, some report the sounds of a woman's screams echoing from the attic, the same room in which Alice Littlefield supposedly had her ordeal with bats. The attic is also noteworthy in that, though unoccupied and without easy access to the turret windows, many have observed the shutters opened at one moment and closed the next.

There have also been reports of objects being moved, as in one case where a pair of candlesticks were found lying in the center of the living room floor. Though they were on the mantle before the doors were locked, and the building empty until the next person with keys came in the next morning, it looked as though they'd been taken down and tossed away.

Also, whether it's a product of the musically-inclined Alice Littlefield or the fact that the Music Department was, at one time, housed here, some have also heard music playing from empty rooms. The music stops upon investigation.

Present Day

The Victorian structure stands, as of this writing, lavishly furnished and active in university life. While the downstairs is unoccupied, the second floor houses the office of Resource Development Special Programs. The downstairs is used for official functions by the president of the university.

It seems that the ghosts have not quieted down, as those who work in the building are eager to share their own brushes with the unexplained. The feelings of dread and other paranormal activities continue, frightening some and amusing others.

While the Littlefield home is a fixture on campus and one of the most breathtaking architectural structures, it is not often opened to the public. Special tours can be arranged, during which the visitor is treated to all the sights of the old building.

†††††

St. Edward's University

3001 South Congress Avenue

Among the faculty, there are priests and laymen guiding the students with firm hands toward their goal of achievement. Students sit on the side of a grassy hill, their thoughts on lessons to be learned during their time here. Others sit in the shade provided by the high Main building. This campus is rich with tradition and history, stretching back nearly 130 years. As with any place of such age, the buildings have seen their share of tragedy...and some shadows run colder than others.

St. Edward's University sprang from humble beginnings a year after the death of Mrs. Mary Doyle, who left most of her 498-acre home to the Catholic Church. Founded by the Reverend Edward Sorin, the school was named for St. Edward, the Confessor and King. Its total student population during its first year, 1878, was three boys. Seven years later, then-president, Reverend P. J. Franciscus, obtained the college's first charter.

It seemed that tragedy marked the campus frequently, as in the case of the strange fire that claimed most of the Main building in 1903 or the freak tornado of 1922, which damaged not only Main, but other parts of the campus as well.

By 1925, St. Edward's gained a university charter. Priests of the Holy Cross made up almost the entire faculty and the school became known for excellence in learning. Its sister school, the Maryhill College for Women Only, was absorbed into the university in 1970. Since then, growth has continued, leading to St. Edward's being referred to as one of the finest private institutions in the world.

As with any campus, however, there are stories that one would hardly expect in the world of academia. Phantom footsteps, priests who disappear before startled eyes, and old students who never left provide a colorful, if macabre, backdrop for incoming students. While many of the stories fall under the banner of urban legend, some prove frighteningly true.

††††††

The Main Building

Looking up at the tall building, it is easy to see that this college is run by priests. After all, the Main building looks less like a schoolhouse than it does a house of God. Stretching high into the sky, its pointed roof and rough-hewn stone walls call out in pious dignity, at once imposing and inspiring. Out of the sunlight, it is apparent that this building remembers its history. Students, faculty, and staff believe that Main holds many echoes of the past...and a few things that simply refuse to leave.

What creates a haunting? Is it the mere age of a building or the rock from which it is built? More likely, it's the emotional turmoil that dwelt within that left scars in the wood and mortar. Though the past is gone, the building never forgets, and often seeks to remind those who take their history for granted.

Its History

Construction on the building now called Main began in the early 1900s—and immediately got off to a bad start. During construction, a family of trick bicycle riders would entertain themselves and others by riding up and down the construction planks. Tragedy struck, when one of the riders slipped off a plank and fell to his death. The building was completed in 1902, but it did not stay up for very long. An unexplained

Main Building, St. Edward's University

fire broke out in 1903, destroying a great bit of the building. It was rebuilt, but in 1922, a freak tornado ripped through the campus, again bringing severe damage to the old building. In both instances, students are reputed to have died.

Death, it seems, lingered in the halls of Main for quite some time. During the 1920s, parts of the building were used as dormitories for brothers and brother-candidates. One such candidate, for unknown reasons, took his own life. A second hung himself in Main's tower.

As late as 2001, the building seemed to continue its strange tradition, claiming the life of a professor of languages who fell from the third floor. The best guess is that, during a windstorm, he reached to close a window and lost his footing.

The Ghosts

With the number of tragedies the building has seen, it is little wonder that it holds a reputation of being haunted. However, these hauntings are no mere product of overactive imaginations. They are, to those who have experienced them, very real. Students, priests, custodians, and laymen have all had their share of experiences, some more frightening than others.

During one period, a section of Main was used as a bookstore. Repeatedly, descriptions of a tall man in what appeared to be a friar's coat were reported. Keys left in doorways would jingle and footsteps could be heard in the otherwise empty room. Though new employees were not informed of the specter, each invariably had their own encounter.

Another strange sighting of a phantom monk occurs right outside the building, where security guards have seen the being disappear. In one instance, a guard claimed to have hit and run over the apparition—only to find no trace of anything in the road.

Other phenomena reported in the old building include strange noises, cold spots, and unaccountable feelings of panic. While some scoff at the notion that such a holy site could possibly be haunted, there are others who will swear to it.

Present Day

Since the building's renovation, there has been little activity from the presence in the former bookstore. A copy center and post office now sits where books and spiral notebooks used to. Still, signs of ghostly activity continues, with items sometimes disappearing and then reappearing in strange places. Sightings of the phantom monks also persist, but not with any real frequency. Most of the activity occurs inside the building, where students will not be found after dark.

The Main building is open during the day to students, as there are many offices and services offered within its walls. At night it is locked up tight, and that is perhaps for the best, as few notice wandering spirits among the other priests and students. But when there are supposed to be none, some encounter the unexpected. Time of year seems to hold no sway over the restless souls, so the best bet of seeing one would be after hours.

†††††

Mary Moody-Northen Theater

Sitting in the seats, waiting for the show to start, patrons are abuzz about the impending performance. Backstage, actors dash about; getting into costume, applying makeup, checking props, and running lines. There is a palpable edge in the air, but to some it is not just the

Mary Moody Northern Theatre

play—it's the notion that around any gather of curtain, or perhaps peering down from the light rigs, something may be watching. It's not the audience that sets nerves jangling, but those who watch for all eternity, staring down upon the actors.

All theaters, it seems, are haunted. Tales among thespians would lead an outsider to believe that they are, if not superstitious, remarkably dramatic. Many theaters have a "patron ghost," or guardian, who is merely a favorite actor or actress—whether or not he or she ever really set foot in the building and whether or not he or she is real or imagined in their ghostly form. In some cases, however, the spirits within theaters are *very real*...frighteningly so.

Its History

Built in the 1960s through a grant from the Mary Moody-Northen foundation, the theater was marked by tragedy early in its existence. During those years, one particular student in the theater, who had great aspirations of becoming a professional actor, was the first to leave his mark. He was, according to college lore, quite talented, but when tragedy struck his personal life in the form of his girlfriend breaking up with him, he took his own life by hanging himself by the sand bag ropes.

It was also during this time period that the second indelible stain marked the theater, this time in the form of a teacher. While little is known about the actual event, the teacher, called "Tom," was reputed to be a homosexual in a time when such a thing was scandalous. For whatever reason, Tom committed suicide, though not in the theater.

The Ghosts

There are three restless souls said to inhabit the theater, two of which have tragic connections to the theater's past.

† The first, and most often sighted, is said to be quite flirtatious with the female students. He enjoys teasing the young women of the theater, stroking their hair or appearing in the women's dressing room. There is little question as to the identity of this specter, as apparitions are accompanied by the shadow of his hanging body by the curtain and the sounds of creaking ropes that are no longer there.

† Though the second spirit did not die in the theater, he so loved it, apparently, that he returns often. Reputed to be the ghost of the teacher named Tom, he is seen most often in the lighting rig, wearing a top hat and tails. He is also said to frequently sit in the audience to watch performances and rehearsals.

† The third spirit said to walk the halls of the theater is the lady for which it is named, Mary Moody-Northen. While her presence may be more a product of the imagination or romance of the theater, there are some who swear her spirit watches over them all.

It is worth noting that no records of any person dying in the theater, by suicide or other means, exist. However, the sightings persist, even by those who do not know the legends.

Present Day

Tales of the theater ghosts are passed from one class to another, with each one adding their own encounters. Classes still continue, as do the sightings.

As the theater is in constant use, the best time to visit is during classes, if one is a student. Then, it is simply a question of keeping one's eyes open for the unexpected. There have never been records kept as to the specific times of year the ghosts walk, but they are most often seen during rehearsals, watching over the players as if waiting for their cues.

6

Haunted Museums and Organizations

One of the best places to go to learn about the culture of a people is a museum. History, it is said, comes alive. What were surely someone's family photos or discarded shawl is put on display, examined for clues about the time from which it came. Questions about the lives that were lived and lost in building the state of Texas can be answered by paying respect to those who came before and looking back at history with a grateful attitude. We can never truly know where we are going as a people, it has also been said, unless we know where we've been. But as true as the figurative old adage may be, there are other places where history does come alive. The items on display may very well represent typical craftsmanship of the time, but they also belonged to people, flesh and bone. No matter what a person touches, a bit is left behind. Sometimes what remains is more than just a scratch or a fingerprint.

There are other places where, though not technically museums, the past meets the present. Asphalt roads and electric lights seem oddly out of place against their walls, and visitors half expect to be taken back to another era when passing through their doors. They are proud buildings, having seen the earliest of days of Austin. Another old adage says, "If only these walls could talk." In Austin, many of them do.

The Neill-Cochran House of Museums

2310 San Gabriel Street

Beneath the high columns and broad porch, one cannot help but be awed by the sheer immensity of the structure. To step through the doorway is to step back in time, visiting images and trappings of the past. No matter where one turns, eyes alight on works of art, carvings of masterful craftsmanship, and furniture the likes of which are not seen in today's modern society. And still, between the spaces of heartbeats, there are other things. Visitors can *see* them, *hear* their cries, and before even breath can be drawn, they are gone. The past is still very much alive here in this structure that has survived for over a century, through war, strife, and even death.

The south is well known for its architecture, particularly during the antebellum time period. Austin may be more distinctive than many others because most of its most famous structures were designed and built by a single man, Abner Cook. However, it's not the construction or the shape of the house that makes it historic, but the times it has seen and the uses it has had—and it's these two things that make this old mansion haunted.

Its History

When the capital of Texas was comfortable in its Austin location, the decision to build permanent government buildings came rapidly. For the most part, Abner Cook, the brilliant architect and designer, was the man of choice for the buildings that were considered most important,

Neill-Cochran House

including the Governor's Mansion. It was in 1855 that a young surveyor named Washington Hill contracted Cook for his new home. Built entirely of native Austin limestone and Bastrop pine, the home became a luxurious testament to Cook's talent. Hill, who was often away on business, trusted that his wife would move into the house on completion. She, however, fearing the Indians that used a nearby trail, refused.

Hill's troubles were just beginning, as he'd overextended himself financially in the purchase of additional acreage. Without means, he was forced to sell his luxurious new home, as well as the surrounding 17.5 acres, and relocate to downtown Austin. The home was purchased in 1856, and became the first home to the Texas Institute for the Blind.

At the end of the Civil War, General George Armstrong Custer commandeered the house and its land as headquarters for United States troops that were to oversee Reconstruction. It was used for, among other things, a military hospital. Many of the soldiers housed in this new stronghold had contracted Yellow Fever and died due to lack of medication.

In 1876, Confederate Colonel Andrew Neill, a native of Scotland who arrived in Texas near the end of the Texas Revolution, purchased the house for himself and his second wife, Jennie Chapman, and their children. When he died in 1883, Chapman, Neill's two children, and a niece remained in the house and maintained an active presence in the Austin social scene.

The family left the house in 1892, but retained ownership while they rented it to Judge Thomas Beuford Cochran and his wife, Elizabeth Rose. The house was so perfect for them and their five children that Cochran bought it outright in 1895. Though the judge died in 1913, the Cochran family continued to inhabit the house until 1958, when it was purchased by the National Society of the Colonial Dames in America in the State of Texas. Through their efforts, the house was reopened as a museum.

The Ghosts

There are several unquiet spirits that wander the grounds of the old mansion.

One has been identified as Colonel Neill, riding his horse over his land during the day and nighttime hours. He is also seen on the front porch, drinking lemonade with a second man who bears an uncanny resemblance to General Robert E. Lee.

The most frequent sightings, however, are also the most tragic. Many visitors have reported seeing men in military uniforms who seem to be suffering. Perhaps these are echoes of the past from when the halls were lined with those afflicted with Yellow Fever. There are also reports of areas in which the air goes cold and the sounds of anguished moaning can be heard. As if verifying the sightings, several sets of bones, presumed left over from when the house was a military hospital, have been found in the yard.

Present Day

The Neill-Cochran House of Museums stands today as a testament to the beauty of old Austin. Each room is decorated in antiques and artwork, and are inspiring to behold. Among the exhibits shown is a collection of antique ladies fans, as well as dresses from the same time period. It exists to foster pride and understanding in the history of the town, and great pains and a considerable amount of work is taken to preserve its historic beauty.

The Neill-Cochran House of Museums is open to guests Wednesdays through Saturdays, from 2 to 5 p.m. Admission, all of which goes to preserving the location, is five dollars per person. Most visits of the paranormal sort, however, happen during the summer months when the air is hot and mosquitoes are thick, and Yellow Fever was at its deadliest.

†††††

For more information about the museum, visit their website at http://www.neill-cochranmuseum.org/. Special tours can be arranged by calling 512-478-2335 in advance.

The Millett Opera House

(The Austin Club)

110 East 9th Street

A t the end of Congress Avenue in Austin sits the massive Capitol building, filling the skyline and drawing the eyes of any who see it. The street, like a tunnel, focuses on the high dome and wide lawn. But for those who know the site, who've seen the stone giant before, there are side streets that contain architecture from a similar

Millett Opera House

time period and with memories to match. One such building exists on 9th Street, quietly awaiting its clientele. And while the building may look out of place or time, situated between a modern storefront and a museum, there is a sense of wonder and pride as one stands in her shadow. It's almost as if she, or someone inside, is watching.

A scant three blocks away from the State Capitol, the Austin Club rests on a quiet one-way street. The beauty and elegance of the building echoes the finely decorated interior, but like all things of its apparent age, it has seen its share of tragedy. While touring Austin, it's easy to follow the main streets with their brightly lit windows and commercial offerings. However, one should always remember that the street not traveled—or seen for that matter—has its own stories and history.

Its History

Where once stood his lumberyard, Charles F. Millett wanted to build the greatest cultural center in the city. He moved his lumberyard to the Colorado River and hired architect Fredrick Ruffini to design the palatial theater, using his own construction firm to fulfill the design. It opened its doors in 1878, with Millett himself taking on the duties of the manager.

Millett, a successful businessman of the day, settled for nothing less than the absolute best in his life—and the opera house that bore his name was no exception. It boasted limestone walls two feet thick, eight hundred moving seats, and boxes for the truly elite. The beauty of the decor was second only to the breathtaking performances by those who performed on its main stage. Among the early performers were John Phillip Sousa, James O'Neill, and Edwin Booth (whose brother John gained a decidedly different sort of fame).

The building was considered the cultural center of Austin, and the second-greatest opera house in Texas, the first being the mammoth Galveston Opera House. Other events occurred at the opera house, including medical shows, political conventions, and even church services. The building was so beautiful, in fact, that the Texas State Legislature decided to use it as a headquarters until the Capitol building was finished.

All good things, however, must come to an end, and so it did for the Millett Opera House. In 1896, a new opera house, one with electric lights, came into existence, driving Millett's house out of business. That same year, Dr. M. A. Taylor purchased the building as a residence. Two months later, the doctor sold the property to his daughter and son-in-law, who turned it into, of all things, a skating rink.

Over the years, the Millett Opera House has held events from artistic to sports, political to private, and was used as public storage for a brief time. However, in 1910, the Knights of Columbus acquired the building and set to work giving it the attention it deserved. It stayed with the organization for nineteen years before changing hands once again, this time to a printing company.

Much of the restoration of the building took place between 1957 and 1979, when the building was owned by the Austin Public Free Schools and leased by an office supply and stationary store. In 1979, the Austin Independent School District allowed a lease, the length of which was fifty years, to the present occupants, the Austin Club.

The Ghosts

Though there is no evidence to support the cause of a haunting, the age of the building, as well as the number of people who've passed through its doors, seems to suggest that, documented or not, it would have seen its share of tragic events. Whether or not an obituary will ever be found, one cannot discount the eyewitness accounts of so many guests and employees who've had encounters with the lady they call "Priscilla."

Exactly who she was is unknown, though there are legends that suggest that she was a performer when the building was still an opera house. The same legend suggests that she fell from above the stage, perishing in the fall. She always appears as a young woman in a flowing white gown, wearing a gold medallion around her neck, most often on the third floor.

Other phenomena reported in the building include cold spots, people and objects being pushed, and the sound of footsteps. She also likes to ride the elevator all through the night and unbind the curtains while no one is around.

Present Day

The Austin Club sets the standard for exclusive elegance in Austin, with luxuriously decorated rooms and private dining. Events are held year-round, providing members with a full social calendar as well as a quiet place to relax. Priscilla, however, needs no membership. She still wanders the halls, startling members and staff alike with her quiet approach and the cold air that precedes her.

The Austin Club is a private organization, allowing access to members only. However, those who simply wish to see the building could drive by any day of the week. The staff is friendly and accommodating, leading one to believe there would never be a bad time at the Austin Club.

††††††

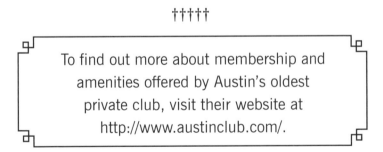

To find out more about membership and amenities offered by Austin's oldest private club, visit their website at http://www.austinclub.com/.

The North-Evans Chateau

(Austin Women's Club)

708 San Antonio Street

Driving through Austin, visitors usually only see the main streets and thoroughfares. The Congress Avenue shops and museums, with their old-style facings, give a glimpse into the past, but often do not do justice to the rich history that the Texas capital holds. Off the main road, onto the side streets, there is little to interest the casual tourist. Rows of apartment buildings and homes line the streets, each with as

The North-Evans Chateau

little character as the last. However, sometimes the side streets hold the unexpected. Turning past the Capitol building, down San Antonio Street, sits just such a surprise in the form of a French-style castle, its face hidden behind a lush canopy of trees. Only when one drives around back can there be a sense of how large the building really is, as it rises high into the sky—and, as with any castle, it seems this building has its share of permanent residents.

The North-Evans Chateau represents a different type of haunting. Whereas most involve some horrific tragedy or even a gentle passing, the majority of hauntings share a common element: someone died within the walls. Not so with the Chateau, as there is no record of anyone having died there, but it seems that a former resident has returned... and never left.

Its History

The North-Evans Chateau began in 1874 as a home, overlooking the Colorado River, for real estate investor Harvey North and his wife, Catherine. They called the home "Bellevue," taken in by the beauty of the unspoiled land around them. The Norths had several children, including a daughter named Athalie Catherine North, who grew up in the house. By all accounts, Athalie was a talented musician who traveled abroad to study her passion. It was on a return trip from Europe that tragedy struck.

On the ship, Athalie took ill with pneumonia; arriving in New York, she was in grave condition. She never recovered, dying in a New York hospital.

In 1894, the Norths sold the Chateau to Major Ira Evans, who hired Alfred Giles to design expansions for the house. Keeping the theme of the French Castle, Giles gave the building its current wide face and dramatic archways. Giles' work is seen throughout Austin, as it was he who designed the original courthouse. Evans lived in the home until 1921, when he moved to San Diego, California, where he died a year later.

The legends surrounding the North-Evans Chateau began shortly after the Austin Women's Club took possession of the building.

The Ghosts

She's seen both day and night by guests and staff alike, and though not everyone has seen her, those who have swear she's real. She appears to waitresses and past presidents. Whether she died there or not, the young woman seen in the halls of the North-Evans Chateau has been identified as Athalie North.

She always appears in a long silk dress and scarf, and always seems to be in a hurry, looking confused and sad. Her appearance has been heralded or accompanied by an icy chill and an overwhelming feeling of despair. Some claim to have had objects moved by unseen hands or even pulled in front of them.

While it is true that Athalie North did not die in the house, the North family sold it soon after her death. Her hurried and confused demeanor make it seem that she returned to see her family...only to find them missing. She now spends eternity searching the house for the family that left long ago.

Present Day

The North-Evans Chateau still stands as beautiful as ever, thanks to the preservation efforts of the Austin Women's Club. It is now a social hub for a great many functions, celebrating Austin women in all fields of business.

The legends continue as well, with sporadic sightings of Athalie. And what do the members of the Austin Women's Club think of their haunted headquarters? They seem to enjoy the history and folklore surrounding their castle. When asked, they treat the stories as if they are the most natural things in the world, and their historian, Donna Hayes, is a fountain of knowledge concerning the house and its origins.

In fact, Ms. Hayes says that if the house isn't really haunted at present, it will be eventually. She fully intends to come back and haunt the house herself. One can only imagine the two women sipping tea together in main parlor.

The staff of the Austin Women's Club is helpful and friendly. Their courteous attitude is extended to all manner of guests during scheduled functions. As there has never been a study of Athalie's appearances for times of year, the best time to visit would be during one of the many soirees held within the castle walls. To reserve one of the beautiful and elegant banquet halls for a private party or a wedding, contact the club's manager, Mark Tidwell, at 512-472-1336.

††††††

To find out more about membership and service of the Austin Women's Club, visit their website at: http://www.austinwc.org/.

7

Guy Town

When researching Austin and the haunted sites within, a pattern emerges. Though, like any city, there are sites at every corner of the metropolis at which the dead refuse to lie still, there is one area that seems to have more restless spirits than its fair share. To walk down that street or drive through that section of town, one might not guess at the history of the place—or to see objects flying off shelves, screaming apparitions, or even hear whispers of those long since gone. In this area, one is more apt to see chic restaurants and politicians on their lunch break. But while, to most people, the area bordered by Fourth Street and the Colorado River means fine dining, it was not always so. One cannot go more than a block or two in any direction without finding an area where the air carries a chill or the shadows dance on their own. In its present incarnation, people are more concerned with spirits of a different kind, but the brick and mortar remembers the times that were and the lives that were often cut short in the area that was once known as "Guy Town."

Much the same as Mexico's "Boy's Town," the Guy Town area held saloons, gambling establishments, and places where, for a fee, a gentleman could obtain the company of a young woman for a brief amount of time. During Austin's infancy, it was said that one could stand on Congress Avenue and at once hear the baying of coyotes, the clicking of billiard balls, and the war cries of Indians. At least the last two could have easily been mistaken for the whoops and raucous laughter coming from the Guy Town district, where the rowdier crowd met to spend their take-home pay.

Due to the nature of the area, fights were nightly occurrences...as were deaths. There is no record of how many died in the establishments, due either to excess or to foul play, but it is known that "Death" was one of the most persistent patrons of the area. Although there were protests by those who disagreed with the lack of morality in the district, Guy Town was tolerated, in no small part because of how popular it was with politicians. In fact, when the legislature was in session, the so-called "female boarding houses" had to hire extra "boarders."

Hard liquor and prostitution were the two main vices indulged in Guy Town, but they were far from the only ones. Gambling was rampant, as was discovered when, during excavations, dice and poker chips were found. There was even a booming opium and cocaine trade going on.

Efforts to close Guy Town were stymied, at least once by the mayor. The district was seen as good for business, attracting new people who would spend their money in Austin. However, in October of 1913, the protesters were heard and the order to shut down Guy Town for good was carried out.

It is little wonder that several buildings in the old district still hold echoes of the past. Though their reputations have long since been changed and the course of business no longer dabbles in vice and excess, the structures bear the scars of what once was the most notorious area in all of Austin.

The Bertram Building

1601 Guadalupe Street

The scents of exotic spices sting the nostrils, making mouths water in hungry anticipation. After being escorted to a table, patrons are treated to the sights and smells of dishes from traditional India. Though the majority of the dinner guests are adults, a lone child is spotted on the second floor looking down, his parents nowhere to be seen. A second glance and the child is gone, probably back to his

The Bertram Building

chaperones. When the evening shift is over and the doors are locked, waitresses and bus boys clean the restaurant, certain that all the patrons have gone. But they cast furtive glances toward the upstairs dining room, where the sounds of laughter and clinking glasses still echo. They smile and nod to each other because they know. It's just another night in historic Austin.

A meal in Austin is not limited to simply Tex-Mex or southern cuisine. Finding foods from cultures from around the world is easy, as the people from those cultures are part of what colors Austin's cultural tapestry. Wherever a person goes, there are secrets to uncover, and there are many tables where the patrons simply refuse to leave.

Its History

The region known as "Guy Town" in Austin was considered one of the most dangerous and exciting areas of the time, but its borders were clearly defined. Just outside its confines, respectable businesses kept respectable clientele, quiet in comparison to their raucous neighbors only one street over. It was in this bordering area that Rudolph Bertram opened his grocery store.

In 1872, Bertram bought the building, using the bottom floor for his businesses and the second floor for living quarters for his family. Among his businesses were a general store and wholesale grocery. He also ran a saloon, but it was distinguishable from those within the Guy Town area in that it was *respectable* and only frequented by the upper class.

It was the respectability of Bertram and his businesses that won him such wealthy clientele and afforded him a comfortable lifestyle. However, even rich men suffer tragedy. Some time between 1880 and 1892, Betram's young son died of Typhoid Fever. Rudolph Bertram grieved the loss of his son until his own passing.

Several years after Bertram's own death, and the closure of Guy Town, the building was purchased. An interesting discovery in the basement gave new perspective to Bertram and his successful business practices, his clientele, and his respectability. Upon investigating the basement, a tunnel was found that led directly to a conveniently placed brothel next door. It soon became apparent that the well-to-do and influential pillars of the community did not want their moral indiscretions known, so they used the proverbial back door. Bertram, in return, saw his business flourish.

The Ghosts

The most common phenomenon in the Bertram building is the sound of a loud spirited party coming from the upstairs area. It seems that the good times and high spirits of the past refuse to let the party die down. Many times, the restaurant staff has gone up to investigate, only to have the sounds stop abruptly when they reach the second floor. The noises begin again when they leave in a darkly humorous game of cat and mouse.

The most disturbing, and tragic, phenomenon to be reported over the years is the apparition of Bertram's son. Patrons and staff alike have reported seeing the child on the second floor, only to have him disappear at the next glance.

Present Day

The Bertram building still sits on Guadalupe, marked as historic for its 150-year existence. It is not, however, denoted for its role in perpetuating Guy Town. Rather, it is marked as part of the historic "Warehouse District," which locals will recognize as much the same thing, and has the salacious nickname of "Whorehouse District."

Over the years it has served as several different restaurants and bars. Though the entrance is still visible, the infamous tunnel to carnal pleasures has long since been blocked off. Today, one is more likely to smell curry than thick perfume in the air, as it now serves Indian cuisine and goes by the name of "The Clay Pit."

Though most of the reports of the ethereal partiers come after closing time, places that do such business as The Clay Pit could have such noises at all hours and just be unaware, as the normal sounds of a day's business could cover any other. The boy, on the other hand, has been spotted throughout the day and night by all kinds of people. There is a sense of sadness that follows him, affecting some who come too close. He stares out through sickly eyes, and some have reported that they could feel his gaze like ice on their necks.

As with any establishment with first-class cuisine, the best time to visit is around dinnertime.

†††††

To find out more about The Clay Pit, their daily lunch buffet menu, or hours of operation, visit them online at http://www.claypit.com, or call 512-322-3151.

The Spaghetti Warehouse

117 West 4th Street

The long red brick building seems unassuming in nighttime Austin. Across the street sits another restaurant, a theater that plays the best of second-run movies, a few bars, and other establishments of the like. But behind the heavy wooden door are things unexpected: tables made of old brass beds and a trolley car that sits in the middle of this large former warehouse, each filled with patrons whose mouths salivate at the spicy scent of fine Italian cooking. Behind the panes of

Spaghetti Warehouse

glass of the old car sits a family whose orders have come and gone… yet still they stay. Cold chills follow patrons toward the restrooms, and even after the doors are locked, the sounds of revelry and merrymaking can be heard by anyone who might be passing by.

Italian food is a hallmark of romantic evenings, as are restaurants with their own distinctive atmospheres. The owners and staff do their best to create an unforgettable dining experience, but some of the most unique occurrences happen long after the last paying customer has gone. And though there is no record of any tragedy in the restaurant, the building is very old—and the souls of those who came before remain to this day.

Its History

As did many structures that stood in the former Warehouse District, the building that is now known as the Spaghetti Warehouse held dual purposes. It was, indeed, a warehouse to those who saw the warehouse district as just that. However, to the denizens of Guy Town, its wares were of a slightly different nature. It is commonly believed that the building also housed a brothel, and that every night the sounds of merriment, and the occasional sounds of fighting and even death, reverberated from the walls until the morning light made the operators return to discretion.

By the time Guy's Town ceased operation, the old warehouse had seen more than its fair share of tragedy. As with any place that trades in vice, the pleasures it dealt were often supplied thanks to the suffering of others. While there are no records of anyone dying in the building, few records of any such events exist for Guy Town. It can be assumed that the ladies did not have the easiest of lives, and were often victimized by their customers.

The Ghosts

There have been several investigations into the paranormal activity at the Old Spaghetti Warehouse. Stories abound in Austin-area newspapers whenever someone mentions ghosts in the state capital, with the restaurant almost always making the list.

Perhaps the most curious soul to be reported is that of a young boy, usually described as being between eight and ten years old. He runs through the building after hours and is most often seen near where the modern restrooms now stand. His identity is unknown, but it's assumed that he was the child of one of the prostitutes who lived in the old warehouse. Though the current manager has never seen him, several former employees say they'll never forget his blond hair and impish giggle as he darted just out of their view.

Another apparition that bears scrutiny concerns the curious centerpiece of the restaurant, an old trolley car that is used for dining. According to published reports, there seems to be an entire family of specters that sit patiently at their table for a meal that will never arrive. Usually after closing, when the dining area has been cleared, an unwary server or busboy will be taken by the feeling of eyes on him. When he looks up, he *sees them*, four faces, staring out from the trolley window.

The most unnerving phenomenon that occurs surrounds the basement storage area. Many of the employees report feelings of dread when they descend the stairs, along with the feeling of being watched. So intense is the feeling... there are several employees who simply will not enter the basement area alone anymore.

Also reported are objects that swing and clatter with no physical source, cold spots, and items that have disappeared completely, only to return later in strange locations. One former employee also reported lights that flickered for no reason, and while faulty wiring may be more at fault than phantoms, the building's eerie reputation didn't diminish the spooky effect. While no one can say for certain who haunts the building, or even why, with any authority, few doubt that it is, in fact, haunted.

Present Day

The Old Spaghetti Warehouse sits today, open for business and serving some of the best pasta in town. Its decor is an eclectic mix, with many of the tables being fashioned from the headboards of old brass beds in what would be a twist of humor. Sitting in the middle of the dining area is the old trolley car, in which couples can sit for at least the illusion of privacy. The scent of fresh bread and tomato sauce always wafts through the air, making it difficult to pass by without feeling hungry. And while current management has never had an experience of the paranormal sort, the haunting persists, according to other employees.

Due to the nature of the haunting and the brisk business of the restaurant, phenomena may occur at all hours and simply go unnoticed. A busy restaurant can, after all, provide many distractions. But, when the rooms are quiet and the guests have gone home, one can take the time to notice an out-of-place child or a family that just refuses to leave. It seems, therefore, that the best time to visit the Old Spaghetti Warehouse is when one wants a fine pasta meal. Just keep your wits about you and your eyes open...because you never know who, or what, could be sitting in the next booth.

††††††

For more information about the
Old Spaghetti Warehouse, their food,
catering, or to download their menu, visit
http://www.meatballs.com.
For reservations, call 512-476-4059.

Mug Shots

407 East 7th Street

It is late. The echoes of "last call" have faded and the last happy soul exits the bar into a waiting cab. It's been a good night, and though the wad of bills from his tip jar gives him a good feeling, the bartender just wants to go home and get a well-earned good night's sleep. As he locks the doors, he catches movement out of the corner of his eye. He turns to see a young woman, dressed in a blue gown, crossing the room behind him. He calls to her that they're closed, but

Mugshots

she pays him no mind as she makes her way to the stairs. He follows, but as she reaches the landing, she turns toward him and promptly vanishes. It's just another sighting of the "Lady in Blue."

A late night in Austin almost always winds up at a bar, where friends get together over a frosty drink to talk about the adventures of the day and to plan new ones for tomorrow. As with most bars, one can usually find all types; college students sit alongside bikers and lawyers as everyone enjoys their evening and winds down after a long day. So many different types are present that it would be difficult to call any of them "out of place." However, in at least one bar in downtown Austin, there is a patron who seems, if not out of place, then out of time whenever she is seen. That may be because she died a very long time ago.

Its History

Little is known about the mysterious lady that haunts the building, only that she wears a blue dress and vanishes before startled people's eyes. But the building in which she appears has a history that, while not definite, could explain her presence.

Late in the 1800s, Austin was a growing city looking to bridge the open gaps between itself and its neighbors. To that end, the building on East 7th Street was built as a headquarters for a stagecoach line that ran between Austin and New Orleans, Louisiana. The line's stable, in fact, sat where now sits "Lovejoys."

Of course, with such close proximity to Guy Town, almost every establishment, no matter how legitimate on the face, had alternative services to offer of one sort or another. While difficult to confirm, the most commonly believed rumor is that the old stage house offered companionship for its weary male travelers in the form of prostitutes that worked out of the top floor.

When Guy Town ceased operations, many of the businesses collapsed. Without their "extra benefits" to offer clients, and with more expedient and modern modes of travel easily available, it is assumed that the old stage line fell by the wayside.

Over the years, the old building has hosted several businesses, most of them bars and restaurants. It was during the reign of one such establishment—the Highlife Cafe—that the legend of the Lady in Blue was born.

The Ghosts

There is another type of spirit that can be found at this bar, and this one doesn't come in a cold glass. Several of the former employees of the Highlife Cafe have had encounters with the lady—and all offer the same account. One employee encountered her as he closed up the bar one night. She slowly walked up the stairs without making a sound. He called out to her that the bar was closed, and in reply, she simply turned and vanished.

Sightings of the lady, however, are not the only phenomena that points to the building being haunted. On one occasion, an owner, having worked late into the morning, grew irritated when the same song played continuously on his jukebox. The song, Oboe Concerto #9, while pleasing to the owner, wasn't the sort of thing he wanted to hear over and over again. Thinking his jukebox broken, he unplugged it and went next door for a cup of coffee. Half an hour later, as he returned to his car, he heard music coming from inside his establishment. The windows were still dark and the front door locked, but from within he could hear the beautiful melody of Oboe Concerto #9.

During its life as the Highlife Cafe, a journalist rented out a private room in the basement for his bachelor party. Among other things, he and his party friends also hired a bevy of exotic dancers to entertain them. During the show, they watched blue lights dancing around the girls and thought it was some portable gadget brought to add to the experience. However, the girls denied having such an item. When the journalist pressed the issue, the lights in the basement went out.

Another well-known sighting involves a group of Highlife Cafe employees who, after dozens of sightings, decided to attempt to contact the Lady in Blue. After trying for hours, including playing the theme to "Alfred Hitchcock Presents," with no results, they gave up. However, as they locked the door behind them, a single plaintive note rang out from the darkened bar.

Present Day

As happens often in Austin, restaurants and bars change hands rapidly. One could conceivably visit several sections of town after only a month and find none of the same establishments. That is most certainly the case with the building at 407 East 7th Street. The Highlife Cafe has long since closed its doors, but the doors were opened again under the name "Mug Shots." A full service bar, Mug Shots caters to those in need of a cold drink to chase away a Texas-sized thirst.

The best time to visit Mug Shots is when one needs something cold and frosty to drink. However, the Lady in Blue is not someone who appears to gawkers. She is most often reported after hours, when the patrons have gone home. But on some nights, passing by, don't be surprised to hear classical music playing from behind the darkened windows. Invariably, it will be the hauntingly beautiful Oboe Concerto #9. The bar may be closed, but the Lady does enjoy her music.

†††††

Mugshots was awarded CitySearch's "Best Bartenders" and "Best Dive Bar" in 2007. To contact the bar, call 512-236-0008.

Bitter End Bistro and Brewery

311 Colorado Avenue

Acid Jazz and a cool vibe can be just the thing to relax after a long day in Austin. A place to meet up with friends, relax, and enjoy some of Austin's best micro-brewed beer sounds like just the thing for street-weary travelers. But there are other spirits than those lifted by the ambiance or those that are poured from a bottle. And, when surprises pop up, the staff just smile and nod, for while moving furniture and roving clouds of moisture may not be the norm at other places, such things are just about a daily occurrence when you travel on the "B-Side."

The Bitter End Bistro and Brewery

People are often known by their associations and the company they keep—and can be haunted by their past. Buildings, it seems, are often the same. Sharing a wall with the famed Old Spaghetti Warehouse, it is little wonder that the past seeps through the walls...or that the souls of those long dead come out and play.

Its History

Though separated in modern times, the Bitter End Bistro and Brewery, as well as the adjoined B-Side Bar, were once part of that most notorious of hotspots in Texas, Austin's Guy Town. During the late 1800s, it was part of the grocery warehouse.

Its history is much the same as its neighbor, with rumors abounding about illegal operations, prostitution, and even a speakeasy that once operated out of the building. When it opened as a microbrewery and restaurant in 1993, the owners knew they were on historic ground. However, it wasn't until three years later that the owners discovered a hidden basement that ran beneath the Bitter End and the Old Spaghetti Warehouse. It seemed that some of the rumors might have been true after all. Due to the presence of only one door—one that only opened on the side of the building—the owners hypothesized that the space was used as one of the fabled speakeasies of the 1920s, with bootleg liquor, illegal gambling, and women for hire.

After the discovery, the owners decided to honor the building's dubious past and opened the "B-Side" addition, a luxuriously decorated space in which customers could enjoy sipping drinks in low light and a fun atmosphere. It was also shortly after the opening of the new bar that strange phenomena began to occur with curious frequency.

The Ghosts

"Oh," says Ryan Fulmer, manager of the establishment. "You want to hear about the ghosts."

He says the phrase in a friendly fashion, but with a hint in his voice that lets you know it's not just the beer that made his establishment famous. In truth, the Bitter End and B-Side are mentioned in almost any guide to haunted Texas, so frequent are the sightings and experiences. In fact, many of the employees refuse to go to the B-Side alone—even during daylight hours.

The most common sighting is of dark shadowy figures that roam the building, often disappearing into the B-Side section before heading through the wall shared by the Spaghetti Warehouse. The figures are often mistaken for bar patrons who have stayed past closing, yet they disappear when followed.

Another manifestation seen by many first began showing itself in 1997. It is a strange gray cloud that forms in one corner, despite there being no vent for condensation or other type of atmospheric discharge, and moves about the bar. When it appears, several of the employees refer to it as "raining" inside, but only in that corner and the walls and ceiling are dry.

There have been other events, less innocuous than a floating cloud of mist. One unfortunate employee, while napping in the upstairs room, suffered from a terrible nightmare in which all his energy was drained. He awoke to find that he could not move and that the normally sweltering room was bitter cold.

One of the more interesting phenomena that occurs is the movement of objects without assistance from any physical hands. On one occasion, a night manager went through his routine of cleaning up the bar and pushing each of the twenty-five barstools under the bar, where they belong. He left the room for only a moment, but when he returned he was startled to find all twenty-five stools had quickly, and noiselessly, scooted back a few feet from the bar. Invisible hooligans have also ransacked storage closets, and many small items have gone missing from the Bitter End, only to turn up in the B-Side area.

Present Day

Employees of the B-Side and Bitter End Bistro and Brewery all know about the phenomena—and tell their stories with eager glee. And while not everyone believes them, it seems that everyone who works in the bar has their own tale to tell. It is open for lunch on weekdays, as well as into the night. Weekends are usually just for the evening crowd.

Though not specific to a time of year, most of the phenomena seem to occur during the times when the old speakeasy would have been in operation, though there have been sightings during broad daylight. It seems that the B-Side half of the establishment is where most of the activity is centered. And while there are never any guarantees about witnessing such an event, at the B-Side, the odds are just about even.

✝✝✝✝✝

For more information about this historic restaurant, call 512-478-BEER.

8

Other Haunted Hotspots

There are, in every city, places that defy description. Neither shop nor restaurant, these places exist both out in the open and hidden away. In many cases, a person might just walk right by without even realizing what they've passed. A building with a closed door, another where suits and ties move in a constant stream, and even places so secluded that, had you not known where to look, you'd never have guessed it was there. But they are there, nonetheless, waiting to be discovered, recognized, and explored. They exist not as tourist attractions, but as reminders of a proud history.

This section presents three places that fit no description and were more than a little difficult to find (though one of them sits right on a busy street). It's important that these, like their more famous brethren, are never forgotten. More specifically, the souls that walked within the walls deserve to be remembered with every bit of the same respect as those in more well-known areas.

Moore's Crossing Bridge
Richard Moya Park

C hildren play on the soccer field during the spring, joggers run along the trail, and each of the modern playgrounds is teeming with kids whose shrieks of laughter and joy fill the air. The dense trees provide just the right amount of shade on a summer day, cooling the air to a tolerable level. But just beyond the happy shouts and picnic baskets, the shadows run just a bit darker, the trees grow denser, and standing in the shadow of the old iron bridge, one can feel a chill in the air. A glance upward reveals a person standing on the bridge, staring down. A second glance...and that person is no longer there. There is something strange in this place of happiness...where an historic monument that was marred by tragedy sits sleeping.

Moore's Crossing Bridge looks a bit out of place in Richard Moya Park. While the majority of the park is either well-manicured nature or the best of modern technology, it stands as a reminder of times gone by. And although this bridge has stood in numerous places, one only needs to climb the steps and stand on its wooden floor in this, its current home, for a glimpse back into the past.

Moore's Crossing Bridge

Its History

First erected in 1884, the bridge now standing in Richard Moya Park originally stood across the Colorado River in Austin, only a few blocks from where the State Capitol Building now stands. For the first two years of its existence, the wrought-iron truss bridge was used as a

toll bridge. It was opened for public use amid great celebration in June of 1886. Then called simply the Citizen Bridge, it remained spanning the Colorado River until it was dismantled in 1910 to make way for a wider structure.

The bridge was not, however, destroyed, or its parts salvaged. The bridge was placed in storage until 1915, when a portion was used to replace a low-water crossing on Onion Creek.

Tragedy struck Texas in September of 1921, in the form of the Great Thrall/Taylor Storm. Austin was flooded with 18.23 inches of water when rain fell for a continuous eighteen-hour stretch. Property damage was considered inestimable, and six deaths were recorded along the creek.

In 1922, the remaining sections of the original bridge were used to replace the Onion Creek overpass. The structure was elevated an additional ten feet to prevent damage from future floods.

The land on which the bridge finally came to rest became known as Moore's Crossing, after a grocer named John Moore built a store there.

There is a legend about the bridge, though historical documents confirming the events have not been found. Where the bridge now stands was, according to the legend and to locals, the area where a relationship between a white man and a black woman turned deadly. Such relationships were not seen as acceptable at the time, especially in the South. When the secret got out, a mob formed and chased the couple onto the bridge, then hanged the man from one of the crossbeams. No mention was ever made of what happened to his unfortunate love.

The Ghosts

Moore's Crossing Bridge has been host to numerous investigations and the subject of many reported sightings. Though not every sighting is the same, most agree that the old iron structure is indeed haunted.

The most common phenomena reported involve seeing people in out-of-date clothing crossing the bridge. Many have seen phantom pedestrians making their way across to an area that is impassible. More astonishing is that the people seem to simply vanish on a second glance. Many have reported several observers on the bridge, only to question where they could have gone, and so quickly. There have even been reports of the curiously dressed fellows waving to people before disappearing before their bewildered eyes. While there has never been any confirmation of the identities of the apparitions, many believe them to be victims of the Great Flood.

There also has never been any confirmation of the cause for the most well known haunting on the bridge, but that does not change the fact that many have seen the hanging man and the woman at his feet. As late as the 1980s, sightings were reported, always of a white man hanging from the metal rigging and a black woman sobbing below him.

Present Day

Moore's Crossing Bridge is no longer accessible by car. There are steps leading up to the old wooden plank floor, and pedestrians may cross at any time.

There is a strange feeling one gets from walking on the bridge. The construction of the floor is disorienting, as none of the planks seem to contain straight lines. Looking down while walking is sure to give a dizzying effect. Several points on the bridge tell its age, as there are a few joints that seem to have buckled slightly, however it does provide an impressive view of the park.

Richard Moya Park is open year-round, with no entrance fees. It is a true public park, but hours are posted on the gate and must be adhered to. During the spring, the park is a perfect place for families to play on a lazy afternoon. However, if it's Moore's Crossing Bridge one is interested in, most sightings occur during the foggy hours of autumn months.

Paggi Blacksmith Shop
David Grimes Photography Studio

503 Neches Street

"There is a black man laughing here," said the psychic. "He never thought he'd be one of his own clients."

All buildings hold remnants of the past within them. The brick, mortar, and steel used in their construction often retain the energy of things long since forgotten, and histories both bright and tragic. No matter what becomes of the structures, the owners find themselves to be the proud owners of sites that bear a greater distinction than simply being "historic." Those sites are haunted.

While walking about the Sixth Street and Warehouse District areas, one can often see the remnants of the past in the faces of new businesses. Some buildings may seem so innocuous that one could walk right by them without even noticing their presence, but behind the front door, the owners tell stories of phantoms and moving shadows. In this city, it is often more difficult to find a building without a history than one that is inhabited by voices from the past who refuse to rest.

Paggi Blacksmith Shop (David Grimes Photography Studio)

Its History

The structure at 503 Neches Street came into being in 1875 as a business venture of Michael Paggi, an Italian businessman of some prominence in Austin. Prior to opening the shop, Paggi's ventures were diverse, beginning in 1870 when he arrived in Austin with two ice-making machines. By 1872, he'd become the superintendent of the Austin Ice Company, but his ventures did not stop there. He owned several shops, in which he sold soda water, syrup, and ice cream. He owned several bathing establishments and set up one shop to sell bathing suits, a strange precursor to modern businesses who do much the same thing to those who enjoy Town Lake and the nearby rivers. He even, at one point, ran what he called a "Mexican Fandango," a contraption consisting of several horses bridled together that marched in a circle for folks to ride.

In 1875, Paggi purchased the land on the corner of Neches Street and built a wagon and carriage sales shop with a blacksmith shop for service. He sold Studebaker wagons, buggies, surreys, and spring wagons, and used the blacksmith shop for repairs and modifications. His business boomed, allowing him to purchase a large house in what was known as "Judge's Hills."

When Paggi died in 1911, the building was sold to an African-American named Nathan Rhambo, who used it as a black mortuary. The only one in the city that catered exclusively to blacks, the funeral parlor made Rhambo a wealthy man. He was well known in the city for wearing only white suits, riding around in a white carriage that was drawn by white horses. He was, by all accounts, very well liked and well known. However, such notoriety in the South was not always a good thing for a black man. On June 20, 1932, Rhambo was called to what is now the Round Rock area, presumably to pick up a body for preparation. He was found the next day in his car, beaten severely and shot in the head. His body was taken back to his own funeral home for preparation. Three men were arrested in the crime, with the fellow who "hired" him dying in the electric chair soon after. While some feel the motive for the murder was robbery, one fact that was mentioned in newspaper reports of the crime indicate that a large diamond ring was still on Rhambo's body when he was discovered. Another theory is that he was killed by men who had heard about the "uppity nigger" and who didn't take kindly to his flaunting his wealth.

The historic building switched hands many times over the next several decades and was in a state of disrepair when a photographer named David Grimes purchased the building in 1993 as his studio.

From the beginning, Grimes knew there was something more to the building than met the eye. He found artifacts from Paggi's shop, including blacksmith tools and bits of twisted metal, writing on walls, and other curiosities during his renovation. But one night, as he was showing a friend his new space, a police officer shined his flashlight through the window and demanded to know what they were doing there. When Grimes explained he was the new owner and invited the officer in to see what they were doing, the policeman smiled and declined. He explained that he'd never set foot in that building...*as it was haunted*.

Other phenomena occurred, one of which involved a friend asking when David hired the "new secretary" who sat in the front room. No such employee existed, and when the room was checked, the woman was gone. After too many phenomena to ignore, Grimes hired a psychic to come and look at the shop. As soon as she entered, she said, "There is a black man laughing here. He never thought he'd be one of his own clients."

The Ghosts

While there is no doubt in Grimes' mind that the building is haunted, the identity of some of the specters remain a mystery. The specter that can be seen out of the corner of one's vision is frequently sighted, as is the silhouette of an old woman in the front doorway. However, if the psychic that Grimes hired is to be believed, it's the soul of Rhambo that still paces the rooms of the house.

In addition to sightings, there are other interesting phenomena that are, to say the least, unsettling. The sounds of shuffling feet from the upstairs beauty salon, after it is closed and locked, are commonly heard. One of the make-up specialists from the business swears she was pushed down the stairs to the second floor by unseen hands.

Grimes' experiences, however, are the most fascinating. One incident involved a remote-controlled car that ran around the main room of the studio, even though there was no one there to control it. On another occasion, Grimes took a glass from his cabinet and watched as it was split neatly into two pieces, as if someone had sliced it with a sword down the middle. Grimes still owns the glass as a reminder of the strange things that can—and often times does—happen in his studio.

Present Day

The Paggi Blacksmith Shop is on the National Register of Historic Places, although there is no marker on the outside of the building. David Grimes still operates his photography business, specializing in commercial photography. He also continues to feel the influence of the past within the walls of his studio. There have been numerous articles in which Grimes has been quoted about working in a haunted location, and the hauntings persist to this day. In fact most everyone who has worked with Grimes in his studio has had some sort of experience, from apparitions of people to strange noises.

Hauntings of the sort that manifest at the old Paggi Blacksmith Shop do not stick to any set schedule. The events appear to be random in occurrence. While Grimes is a personable fellow, who is willing to talk about his paranormal experiences, one must remember that his studio is a functioning business, and for Grimes, business is good.

To find out more about David Grimes, see samples of his photography, and even to read a few personal ghost story accounts, visit David at his website, http://www.davidgrimes.com.

The Littlefield Building

Corner of 6th Street and Congress Avenue

Walking past the Driskill Hotel, one can feel a chill in the air. Wherever the shadow of the structure kisses the ground, it is as if eyes of ice stare down. Most quicken their pace, anxious to get out from under the stony gaze. They cross the Sixth and Congress intersection, where the warmth of the sun gives welcome relief, but as they step up onto the sidewalk, the cold feeling returns. The shadows of a second monolithic building have the same icy stare, and while what lurks inside is not known, one can be certain that this building has quite a story to tell.

In Texas, there is a saying that often starts with: "You can't go three feet without…" Most of the time, that saying is an exaggeration on the frequency of coffee shops or tourist traps. However, on 6th Street, there *really* are places where you can't go more than a block without running into another haunted building. And while some of these buildings would not make a person glance twice, as they look as innocent as most of the others in town, there are a few that, even were they not haunted, would make most people stop and take notice. Such is the case of the historic Littlefield Building.

Its History

At nine stories tall, the Littlefield building towers over the street with a commanding presence. Its opulent design came about from an equally flamboyant man: banker, entrepreneur, and Major, George

The Littlefield Building

Littlefield. A trustee of the National Bank, Littlefield was well known for being headstrong, as well as being a man who got what he wanted. Between the years of 1895 and 1903, Littlefield actually owned the Driskill Hotel and used part of the structure to house his newly-formed American National Bank. By 1910, Littlefield decided he needed a larger space for the bank and he wanted the space to be close by, so he promptly had the neighboring Ziller building demolished to make way for one of his own design.

Lavish in construction, the building featured two electric elevators, hot and cold water, and an interior decorated entirely in pink marble. When it was finished in 1912, it was eight stories tall with a Japanese-inspired garden on the roof, which was to be used for formal soirees. It opened to a great deal of fanfare, as its 1912 opening featured two reels of moving pictures, orchestral music, a procession of little girls with their dollies in decorated carriages, and a searchlight that could be seen for twelve miles. However, Littlefield realized, his building was shorter than his across-the-street competitor, the Scarborough building, so he had the top garden enclosed, adding a ninth floor and Turkish and Russian baths for good measure. His renovations allowed him to accurately claim that his was the tallest skyscraper between New Orleans and San Francisco. The ground floor contained six storefronts, the bank, a billiard parlor, and a barbershop.

Major Littlefield became well known in the Austin area as a philanthropist, becoming the single largest donor to the University of Texas.

Over the years, the building has become the hub of financial business in Austin, and has housed offices that dealt in real estate and architecture, as well as numerous attorneys and doctors. Other offices have been occupied by the Austin Public Works Administration, the Texas Liquor Control Board, and the Texas Racing Commission. Perhaps the most famous former tenant was a fellow named Lyndon Baines Johnson, who occupied an office when he was appointed State Director for the National Youth Association.

Major Littlefield died November 10, 1920 and was buried in the Oakwood Cemetery, between his wife and his longtime servant.

The Ghosts

Rumors as to who, or what, may be haunting the Littlefield building cannot be confirmed. While some theories place the identity of the specter as Major Littlefield himself, others say it is the ghost of former President Lyndon Baines Johnson that roams his former office. One theory even claims that the ghosts from the Driskill, next door, are simply paying a visit.

Whatever the case, there are strange things that happen in the building that are difficult to explain. Former tenants talk of cold spots and feeling as if they're being watched as they walk the halls. Elevators have been reported to run by themselves and then quit for no apparent reason. There have also been reports of footsteps being heard on empty floors.

Present Day

The Littlefield building today offers luxury commercial space in the form of 336 offices, several of which are suites. There is a mission-style grill and restaurant in the basement, and it is still the hub of business activity in Austin. The two-ton solid brass doors that once hung at the Congress Avenue entrance are now displayed at the University of Texas' Ashbell Smith Hall. And while reports of paranormal phenomena are few, there have been occurrences as late as 2001.

As with any building such as the Littlefield, its businesses are varied and always in operation. It's locked up at night, providing little opportunity for any sort of paranormal investigation.

9

The Haunted Street

The Source of Trouble

6th Street Area

Walking down Sixth Street, one can be easily taken in by the neon lights and live music for which the area is famous. While infectious grooves fill the air, it's easy to see why Austin, particularly Sixth Street, is often referred to as the live music capital of the world. From college students to businessmen, everyone on the strip seems relaxed and happy and bent on having a good time. But behind the bars, within the darkened alleys, there are shadows...echoes of the past that tell of one of the darkest years in the history of Austin. It was an end to innocence and left scars upon the street and soil as the gutters ran with blood spilled by a madman.

Its History

By the winter of 1884, Austin was a booming city of prosperity where crime, outside the notorious Guy Town, was relatively unheard of. While there were occasionally petty thefts and a few fights, the crimes committed were, on the whole, innocuous. However, the newspaper headlines of December 31, 1884, signaled a change that altered the town for years to come.

"Bloody Work!" screamed the headlines that detailed the death of a young serving girl named Mollie Smith. She'd been discovered behind 901 West Pecan Street, which is now 6th Street, murdered in a brutal fashion; killed with an axe, she had a large gaping hole in her head and had been molested.

The effect of the murder on the streets of Austin was immediate, with people suddenly locking their doors and windows and refusing to go out at night. However, as is often the case, it wasn't the well-to-do that fell victim, but those whose jobs it was to go out into the darkened streets.

In May of 1885, another girl, Eliza Shelley, was found at the corner of what is now Cypress and San Jacinto Streets, murdered with equal brutality. She'd been sexually assaulted after she'd been killed. It was only three weeks until the killer struck again, this time scalping a woman named Irene Cross. *The Austin Daily Statesman*, the newspaper of the day, dubbed the madman "The Servant Girl Annihilator."

In August of 1885, the murders took a bizarre turn, as it became apparent that even those who stayed in their own houses at night were not safe. A servant's daughter, named Mary Ramey, was dragged from her bed to a backyard washhouse where she was stabbed through the ear with an iron rod and raped. She was only eleven years old.

The killer increased his activity in September of that same year, this time breaking into a small house occupied by servants. He managed to get into the house and struck all four occupants in the head with an axe. He then took one of the women, Gracie Vance, out a window, dragged her through weeds and across a vacant lot to a rear stable. Vance apparently recovered enough to fight her attacker, but in vain. He overpowered her and smashed her head with a brick, then raped her. In the cabin, two others, Orange Washington and Patsie Gibson, lay dead. Only Lucinda Boddy survived to alert her employer, but as she lit a lamp in the cabin and discovered her dead housemates, the killer returned and cursed the woman, ordering her to put out the light. Lucinda ran screaming from the building, pursued by the killer. As she struggled, her employer came out with a shotgun, frightening the killer away.

Up until the murders of Orange Washington and company, the killer seemed to prefer black women, with Orange being the only man killed. However, on Christmas eve of 1885, terror rocked Austin, as a woman named Sue Hancock, who was described as one of the most genteel and refined ladies of Austin society, was brutally murdered in her own back yard. Her husband discovered her body, her head having been split open by an axe and an iron rod jammed through her ears in a grisly reminder of young Mary Ramey.

Only one hour later, another white woman—Eula Phillips—was murdered in the wealthiest neighborhood in the city. She was found in an unlit alley behind her father-in-law's home, naked, her head bashed in with the blunt side of an axe. She had been raped as well, an act people now knew to be the calling card of the killer. Her husband was found lying in their bed in the house, an axe wound on the back of his head, still alive.

Though the Governor offered a reward of $300 for the capture of the monster, he seemed to simply vanish. To this day, the murders are unsolved. The city erected the "Moonlight Towers," a group of large lamps to keep the populated areas of the city illuminated, in 1895 so people could feel safe being out after sundown. The city, however, never recovered. Austin's citizens regarded newcomers with a wary eye, with mistrust spreading through the streets like wildfire.

The Ghosts

Though there are no confirmed reports, there are many who say the screams of the women can be heard still at the sites of their deaths.

> † Standing on the corner of San Jacinto and Cypress Streets, one can feel a chill that ghost hunters call a "cold spot," during the month of May.
>
> † The same can be said about the location of the first killing, near Buffalo Billiards and the Driskill Hotel on 6th Street.
>
> † One can also feel the echoes of the past along Town Lake, where the Four Seasons Hotel stands on San Jacinto, the site where Sue Hancock met her demise.
>
> † Even the killer's bloody hands mark the area near the Austin Public Library, as it stands near the spot where Eula Phillips breathed her last.

Present Day

It's interesting to note that many of the details of these horrific crimes were largely forgotten, swept under the streets. It wasn't until 1985, one hundred years after the death of the last victim, that research done by Clayton Stapleton in his book, *What Was Then*, through old newspaper clippings discovered the gruesome history. And while some Austinites wish not to remember, others could never forget. The women's killer was never punished, and their bodies lie in uneasy graves in Oakwood Cemetery.

Only two years after the final murder, another killer struck in London, one who went by the name of Jack the Ripper. Ship records show an Austin connection in the form of a Malay cook named "Maurice," whose arrival and departure in Austin seem to coincide with the murders and whose arrival in Whitechapel seems to correspond to the first activities of Spring-Heeled Jack. No connection was ever proven, however, and many scoff at the idea of the two killers being one in the same, as their modus-operandi were so completely different. Still, standing as reminders of that loss of innocence, Austin's "Moonlight Towers" watch over the city, illuminating areas as they have since the murders. Though only seventeen of the original thirty-one still exist, they still cast light on the nighttime city, attempting to keep the unsavory element to the shadows so decent people can go out into the light.

Most apparitions and phenomena are reported on the anniversaries of the respective deaths, which makes tracking the killer a yearlong prospect. However, if one wants to see the original reports, they'd only have to look through the archives of the *Austin American Statesman*.

†††††

To find out more about this bizarre chapter in Austin's history, visit Clayton Stapleton at his website, http://www.whatwasthen.com.

Afterword

Well, that ends the "tour" of Austin. I hope you enjoyed reading about these places and their ghosts as much as I've enjoyed writing about them.

I've been to some really interesting places all around the country. I've met ghosts in Pittsburgh and New Mexico, and everywhere in between. I've climbed reputedly haunted mountains and visited haunted theaters, dined with the dead in New Orleans and chased them down in abandoned hospitals. It's not something I have a burning need to do, or something I feel "pulled" toward, it's just something I really enjoy, something that fascinates me.

As I said in the Foreword, Austin is a fantastic city. There is always something to do, a band to hear, a restaurant to try. But more than that, Austin is about its living history, as well as moving forward. Cities that can easily blend what was and what is are rare, and Austin does the job nicely. For all the legends that exist in Austin's past, new ones are being made every day.

Whether or not you believe in ghosts, for whatever reason, the undeniable remains that these stories should never be forgotten. They are as much a part of the history and culture of Austin as its people. And, I have to admit, researching them has allowed me to see some really interesting thing and some wonderful folks.

The next time you drive downtown, or walk along 6th Street, or pass by some innocuous building, look around. Enjoy the architecture, and everything the modern world presents about it, but never forget those who came before and those who made Austin what it is today.